UNDERSTANDING THE TOOLS OF THE DEVIL

BY LEBOGANG MERRIAM SEOKETSA

1

DEDICATION

Praise the Lord

I would like to honor and praise God, my Lord and Savior Jesus and the Holy Spirit who is my Teacher, my Helper, my guider and my Advocate for helping me to write this second book.

I would like to thank God and dedicate this book:

To my parents; my husband – Monty Seoketsa, my daughters – Dipolelo,and Bria and my brother David and his daughter Koketso.

To the mothers who always pray for me: Mrs. Joyce Molepo, Mrs. Anna Monama, Mrs. Queen Skosana.

To all members of our ministry "Your Burden is my Burden."

To my Pastor and Spiritual Father of House of Praise Church: Pastor TL Toka and his wife- Yvonne Toka

To my Pastors and Lecturers of International Pentecostal Bible Institute: Pastor Pretorius, Pastor Mofomme and Pastor Phefadu.

To my Pastor, advisor and my well-wisher of The Fountain of Praise and Worship Church: Pastor MS Mogoane and his wife. (Always there)

ACKNOWLDEGEMENT

Without the help of the Holy Spirit who was promised to us by our Lord Jesus Christ, nothing in life can be successful. This is the result of the contribution of many individuals who directly and indirectly share their gifts, talents and not forgetting wisdom of which our Lord said in James 1:5 "If any of you lacks wisdom, he should ask God, who gives generously to all without finding fault, and it will be given to him."

I wish to thank my husband, Monty, and our daughters Dipolelo and Remoikantse for their love, patience (fruit of the Spirit) and understanding for staying long hours on the computer, late nights and early mornings writing. This achievement is also yours.

Special thanks to Pastor MS Mogoane again for listening when I always come to him for advises.

ABOUT THE AUTHOR

Dr. Lebogang Merriam Seoketsa is married to Mr. Monty Seoketsa and they are blessed with two daughters. She earned her Doctor of Ministry from Team Impact Christian University and M-Tech in Public Management from Tshwane University of Technology. She is currently working as departmental administrator and she worked as part-time lecturer in the department of Public Management - Tshwane University of Technology. She worked with different committees in different projects. She taught about deliverance to different groups. She is the founder of the ministry "Your Burden is my Burden" (Galatians 6:2). The ministry is taking care of the needy families. "I am holding on to the Word of God to carry the Great Commission."

The book Understanding the Tools /Weapons of the devil was written by the author after realizing how Christians are

4

tormented by holding on things of the past. Things that hurt them long ago. Sins that are regarded as small but making impact on their lives. Unconfessed sins that the Devil claim as his legal rights.

This book was written to remind the Christians about our God who is unchanging. Our Lord who is not a person that He can tell lie. If He forgave our sins, it is done; we are forgiven saints not forgiven sinners. We become new creation 2 Corinthians 5:17 "Therefore, if anyone is in Chris, he is a new creation; the old has gone, the new has come."

The Devil is on duty on daily basis trying to get Christians in order to torment them. Sometimes people are deceived because they are promised luxurious things and better life. People think that when somebody is owns beautiful cars, big houses and having lot of money, it is the true good life.

This book was written to help some Christians and others that the only good life is Jesus Christ. Jesus Christ is the way; the truth and the life. We are His ambassador. The Bible teaches us that "But seek first His kingdom and His righteousness, and all these things will be given to you as well" (Matthew 6:33). Christians must know that righteousness has nothing in common with wickedness. Light cannot fellowship with darkness and there is no harmony between Christ and Belial.

2 Corinthians 6:14-15. Verse 17 of this says "Therefore come out from them and be separate. Says the Lord. I will be a Father to you and you will be my sons and daughters, says the Lord Almighty."

God is prepared to bless us according to His riches in glory.

PREFACE

This book is about the tools or weapons that the Devil uses to torment Christians on everyday life. It is about the pride that caused him to be thrown out from heaven to hell after he tried to take the position of God.

The bitterness and anger that were in him made him to hold on unforgiveness. Unforgiveness is a poison that kills the person who does not want to forgive with the intentions of killing someone. The problem is that the person holding on unforgiveness is the one who dies slowly not being aware of the death.

Satanic soul ties torment many people and until people accept Lord Jesus Christ as their personal Lord and Savior and renounce these soul ties, the Devil will never leave them. This book teaches people about these soul ties and how one can renounce them. The only soul tie that is accepted by our God is the one of married couples. That one is Godly soul tie.

The Devil always likes to claim his rights from people. If Christians have sins that are unconfessed or they are still holding on some idols, the Devil will claim those as his legal rights. This book was written to help Christians to check on those things and get rid of them.

This book teaches Christians on how to handle the issue of money. People think that money is the only means to take someone somewhere. The earth is of the Lord's and everything in it, including money. Seek the Kingdom of God and His righteousness, the rest will be given to us including money. (Psalm 24:1 and Matthew 6:33).

Praise, worship and prayers open the gates of prisons, release people from bondage, untie the satanic soul ties and set the captive free.

And Jesus said "I saw the Devil falling like a lightning from heaven. I have given you authority to trample on snakes and scorpions and to overcome all the power of the enemy; nothing will harm" (Luke 10:18-19).

TABLE OF CONTENT

UNDERSTANDING THE TOOLS OF THE DEVIL

INTRODUCTION

The tools or the weapons that the Devil uses to destroy Christians are many and varied. He uses these deadly weapons in fighting man and God. Nevertheless, let me tell you this: "there is nothing on earth that can overpower God." When people die or are tormented by the devil with his weapons, the devil deceives himself that he is the winner. The devil cannot be the winner. He lost for the very first time when he was thrown from heaven to the hell. Jesus Christ defeated him once and for all on the cross and it was done.

Christians also have the weapons but the most unfortunate part is that they do not understand the weapons God gave them to fight the Devil. Christians do not trust that God has already conquered the devil for them. They fail to understand these weapons. **Ephesians 6:10-18:** "Finally; be strong in the Lord and in His mighty power. Put on the full amour of God so that they you can take your stand against the devil's schemes." The devil has schemes that he uses to get at Christians. The Word of God advises us to put on the full amour of God. It is dangerous not to put on the full amour. The soldier cannot expect to win the fight without wearing the full amour for protection. By full amour it means everything that is needed for protection in the fight must be put on. There is the full amour of God and the amour of the earth. We must put on the full amour of God. That is the spiritual amour.

Ephesians 6:12: "For our struggle is not against flesh and blood, but against the rulers, against the authorities, against the spiritual forces of evil in the heavenly realms." We cannot put on the earthly weapons when we fight with spiritual forces in the heavenly realms. By flesh and blood is meant we are not fighting with flesh and blood of our brothers and sisters. We are fighting with the forces that use them. Hence we are to put on the amour of God.

Ephesians 6:13 "Therefore put on full amour of God, so that when the day of evil comes, you may be able to stand your ground, and after you have done everything, to stand." Nobody knows when the day of the evil will come. That is why it is important to put on the full amour of God to be ready at all the times. The danger of not putting on the full amour is the one that the devil will not inform us when he comes to rob us.

Ephesians 6:14 "Stand firm then, with the belt of truth buckled around your waist, with the breastplate of righteousness in place," The set truth is that the children of God are free. If someone grabs you by the belt, he can pull you to wherever he wants. Now the good part is, if he grabs us by the belt of the truth, there is nowhere he can take us, because we will be free from his evil tricks. If the devil tries to punch us on the breast, we will be protected by the breastplate of righteousness and Lord will reward us. **1 Samuel 26:23** "The Lord rewards every man for his righteousness and faithfulness. The Lord delivered you into my hands today, but I would not lay a hand on the Lord's anointed." For our righteousness and faithfulness we will be rewarded by God.

Ephesians 6:15 "and with your feet fitted with the readiness that comes from the gospel of peace." … God hates the feet that are quick to rush into evil" (**Proverbs 6:18**).

Ephesians 6:16 "In addition to all this, take up the shield of faith, with which you can extinguish all the flaming arrows of the evil one." The Lord rewards every man for his righteousness and faithfulness. Faith is the weapon that Christian must use to defeat the devil from the spirit of fear. Jesus Christ told his disciples to be happy if they can have the faith like a mustard seed. Because by that kind of faith they can remove mountains or command the sycamine tree (a type of mulberry tree) to move from where is to another place. **Luke 17:6** (**KJV**) "And the Lord said, If ye had faith as a grain of mustard seed, ye might say unto this sycamine tree, Be thou plucked up by the root, and be thou planted in the sea; and it should obey you."

Ephesians 6:17 "Take the helmet of salvation and the sword of the Spirit, which is the Word of GOD." Helmet is what we put on our heads. When we look at the person we start from the head. With the helmet of salvation on our heads the devil will be shaken. The devil will understand that the person with the helmet of salvation must have the sword of the Spirit. What we must understand is that we can have the sword of the Spirit but not knowing how to use it. **Joshua 1:8** "Do not let this Book of the law depart from your mouth, meditate on it day and night, so that you may be careful to do everything written in it." Reading the Word of God daily and meditating on it, will be a help to us to understand how to do everything mentioned in it – the Word of God.

Ephesians 6:18 "And pray in the Spirit on all occasions with all kinds of prayers and requests. With this in mind, be alert and always keep on praying for all saints." Prayer knocks the devil down. Praying in the Spirit on all occasions with all kind of prayers and requests will build the wall of fire that will never allow devil to come near us. The Word of God advises us to request anything in the name of Jesus Christ. When we present all kinds of prayer and request to our Lord, we will be answered. **John 16:22** "Until now you have not asked for anything in my name. Ask and you will receive, and your joy will be completed."

As mentioned above, the devil has many weapons/tools, few will be discussed in this book. The weapons which are going to be discussed in this book are those that the devil is sure of when he wants to knock down Christians. The devil uses different tools in different people. There are some tools that he knows very well that they will not benefit him when he uses them on some people and there are some he knows that they work well.

Holy Spirit is pure and holy. No demon or even the devil can stand for the fire of the Holy Spirit. Where the Holy Spirit is, demons run away, because they burn like the way they torment people. Because of ignorance, Christians are tormented by these weapons.

Chapter one of this book will describe Lucifer (devil) and how he fell from heaven.

Chapter two will discuss the first weapon that the devil uses in Christians because this weapon is the one that made him fall from heaven – pride.

Chapter three will discuss the weapon that made him angry and made him decide that he will never forgive God for what He did to him. The devil forgot that he wanted to take the Kingdom of God. No person will be happy after realizing that one wants to take his position. That weapon is unforgiveness.

Chapter four will discuss the fruit of unforgiveness. This is a powerful tool for the devil because it has fruits that produce sicknesses to people. That is bitterness, anger and hatred.

Chapter five will discuss bondage. Christians are in bondage and they think they are living defeated lives. Jesus Christ defeated all problems for us on the cross. No Christian is allowed or must allow him/herself to listen to the devil when he deceives them that they are nothing. Such bondage are strongholds, soul ties, and legal rights.

Christians must understand that the devil has never won a battle fought strictly within the spiritual realm. His reign over the world system is dependent upon the weakness of human nature, the power of sin, and fear of death.

Chapter six will discuss strongholds and how are they established in our lives. Chapter seven will describe soul ties and how they can be destroyed. Chapter eight will discuss the devil's legal rights. These rights make Satan to be proud that he has rights on Christians who are still giving him chance in their lives. Chapter nine will be about how the love of money hinders our prayers.

Understanding these weapons will bring peace, joy and patience to Christians. Christians will fellowship with God being full of love. The battle has been waged since before the foundation of the world.

Jesus Christ has won the victory for us on the cross and out of an empty tomb. What Christians must be aware of is that as the devil sees that his time is growing shorter, he will enforce his strategies to win more people.

As we are getting into this journey of understanding the tools of the devil, we ask God to help us to respond to the teachings. Let our ears not be dumb for what God is saying to us about this book.

*"Dear Heavenly Father, as you teach me about the tools of the devil, I thank you for this opportunity and ask You to give me revelation knowledge. Please Lord; open my ears spiritually so that I can hear when you teach me through this book. Open my eyes so that I can see all good things you want to show me about this. I am asking wisdom from you in the name of Jesus' Christ because in your Word you said "if we lack wisdom we must ask" (**James 1:5**). Holy Spirit I am asking you to teach me because you are our Teacher and helper. I am asking these in the name of our Lord and Saviour Jesus Christ, Amen*

CHAPTER ONE

LUCIFER: THE BEGINNING OF THE ETERNAL REBELLION

Genesis 1:1 "In the beginning God created the heavens and the earth". Time was divided into compartments as, "morning and evening". When it says "In the beginning God created heavens" the word Heavens is in a plural form and it includes the whole of heaven and all its innumerable parts. This includes the angels, the throne of God, and everything therein. The angles were created at the same time as the heaven, but they are not eternal. Only God is eternal. Even his throne is not eternal because if everything was eternal it would be equal to God.

LUCIFER AND THE ENTERNAL REBELLION

God created angels along with the heavens. The word angel is derived from the Greek word 'angelos' and it means a messenger. The angels have inconceivable power but not omnipotent power, **2 Kings 19:35** "That night the angel of the Lord went out and struck down 185 000 in the camp of the Assyrians." Their wisdom is extensive but not omniscient, **2 Samuel 14:20** "Joab your servant has done this to address the issue indirectly, but my lord has wisdom like the wisdom of the **Angel of God, knowing everything on earth."** The number of angels is great but not limitless (**Hebrew 12:22**). The angels are greater than man because God created man just a "little lower than the angels (**Hebrew 2:7**) - "You made him (the man) lower than the angels."

These beings were created by God to serve Him and be about His throne perpetually. Only three are specifically named in Scripture: Lucifer, Michael and Gabriel. Lucifer apparently was the leader among the other angels and was even called the "anointed cherub" (**Ezekiel 28:14**). His name means "morning star." In his original state, Lucifer was incredibly wise and perfect in "beauty". He was compared to the beauty of a variety of valuable gemstones.

Lucifer, the highest of angels, was the "anointed cherub." His glory sat as a crown above the head of God. Lucifer created lower than God was not satisfied with his position; he desired something higher.

Lucifer was the most beautiful angel. Thou he was wise, his wisdom reminded him of his limitation. He wanted to be like God. Lucifer had feelings of pride because of his exalted position. Lucifer was not satisfied with serving God; he desired equality with God.

THE CHARACTER OF LUCIFER'S RISE AND FALL

Lucifer's fall occurred before the seven days of Creation. Lucifer's fall brought the entrance of sin into the perfect Creation of God. Blinded by pride, Lucifer attempted to take the place of God for himself and rule over the entire Creation.

THE FALL OF SATAN

Isaiah 14:12-15 : I will ..... take God's place

Acts 1:9-11 – Ascend into heaven: Lucifer's first attempt involved his ascent into the abode of God. He wanted to ascend above his position. He moved into the third heaven, the dwelling place of God. He wanted God's place in the throne room.

Revelation 22:1 – Exalt my throne: Lucifer wanted to be exalted above the stars. The term star is often used in Scripture to represent angels (**Rev. 1:20; 12:4**). Lucifer wanted to rule over Michael and Gabriel. This move would make him the ultimate in heaven, perhaps taking the place of God over the angels.

Isaiah 2:1-4 – Govern heaven: Lucifer desired to "sit also upon the mount of the congregation, in the sides of the north". Lucifer seemed to be saying, "I want a share in the kingdom." The problem was that he wanted God's share.

18

Philippians 2:9 – Ascend above the heights: Lucifer's desire was not simply to get closer to God but to surpass God. He sought glory for himself that surpassed the glory of God.

Genesis 14:19-22 – Be like the Most High: The most High (Elohim) describes God as possessor of heaven and earth (Gen 14:19. Lucifer wanted God's possessions. By becoming like the Most High, he would be the possessor of heaven and earth. To be God means nothing is equal to you. God the all-knowing Person, knew Lucifer's rebellious desires and he thought of them. He knew Lucifer's disobedient actions as he did them. God the holy and just One had to punish that which was contrary to His plan. God cast Lucifer out of heaven. Those angels that followed Lucifer were judged with him. The angels that obeyed God and repudiated were rewarded.

God judged the angels who refused to remain in their state. He created a burning hell for Lucifer and the angels who rebelled against Him. Those angels who obeyed God were frozen in perpetual service. They would never be tempted to disobey.

God created man. Then the angels asked, "what if man rebels". There is risk of freedom and God knew when He created free man, that man could not handle freedom. God knew man would rebel and that He would have to punish man as He had punished the fallen angels.

"Is the risk worth it" asked the angels.

God wanted man to worship Him and worship is nothing when it is forced. God loved and wanted a man who could love Him in return.

"What if free man chooses not to worship God?" again the angels asked.

God will shower His love on man in giving him rain for food and sun for strength. God will give him intelligence to provide for his needs.

"Is this enough to get man's loyalty?" again the angels asked. : God will speak to man through conscience. Man's conscience will let him know what to do and avoid.

"Why will God do all this for man?" finally the angels asked. : God the Creator made man and gave him life and opportunity to worship God. But man continually rebels. After man rebelled against God, God gave him another opportunity to be saved and worship the Lord. God's son would be judged in the place of man. "For God so loved the world that He gave His only begotten Son, that whoever believes in Him should not perish but have everlasting life" (John 3:16)

Three prominent factors were present within Lucifer's mind as he sought to unlawfully ascend to the highest throne in the heavens.

1. **Pride:** His ambitious pride in his God-given splendour convinced him that he was worthy of Gods throne and glory.

2. **Unbelief:** His unbelief resulted in failing to believe that God would really punish him if he committed a sin.

3. **Thoughts of self-grandeur were undoubtedly his enemy:** He deceived himself into believing that he could actually wrest the throne of God away from the Almighty. With blinded confidence, Lucifer and his host of rebel angels moved on the throne, only to be met with a barrage of divine judgments.

Let us pray: Dear heavenly Father, I adore you and I will praise you in all days of my life. I understand that the devil has been defeated and I am asking You to help me not to fall into his traps. Thank you for explaining to me how he fell from heaven. Thank You for giving me his picture and for giving me this opportunity of learning about his weapons so that I can also help others about his tricks. I thank you and I love in Jesus Name, Amen.

CHAPTER TWO

PRIDE

Proverbs 6:16 (KJV) "These six things doth the LORD hate: yea, seven are an abomination unto him: **A proud look**, a lying tongue, and hands that shed innocent blood, An heart that deviseth wicked imaginations, feet that be swift in running to mischief, A false witness that speaketh lies, and he that soweth discord among brethren."

Pride and lies are two of the devil's chief tools that were evidenced even in the very beginning. In the first temptation, he lied to Eve and also appealed to human pride. He is the father of lies (**wiki.answeres.com**). Pride is another attribute of the Devil. Pride is the Devil's original sin. From the discussion in chapter one, this pride is directed towards his own beauty. Many people today are badly affected with this pride of the devil. Everybody today is seeking to be more beautiful than ever before. People want more expensive clothes and homes than ever. All luxurious things like never before. Please take note: there is nothing wrong in all these things, but the problem is; we want them over our God Almighty. We want them so badly that we are unable to serve God if we do not have them. We want them to such an extent that we forget God. There is no evil in these things themselves, but the lust for them is a problem.

God hates pride. **James 4:6** "But He gives us more grace. That is why Scripture says: 'God opposes the proud but gives grace to the humble.'" Pride is the first and the most expensive tool that the Devil uses because it is the one that caused him to be thrown from heaven into hell. **Isaiah 14:12-15** "How you are fallen from heaven, O shining star, son of the morning! You have been thrown down to the earth, you who destroyed the nations of the world. For you said to yourself, 'I will ascend to heaven and set my throne above God's stars. I will preside on the mountain of the gods far away in the north. I will climb to the highest heavens, and be like the Most High. Instead, you will be brought down to the place of the dead, down to its lowest depths."

God hates pride because it makes people deceive themselves. "In his pride, the wicked do not seek Him; in his thoughts there is no room for God" (**Psalm 10:4**). Pride keeps many people from acknowledging their sins and accepting Lord Jesus as personal Lord and Saviour. Pride makes us think that we can do everything for ourselves better than others. It makes us think that we do not need God. It hardens the minds and the hearts of people not to hear or take any advice from anyone.

It is pride that makes some people think that they are wise enough to go to church or to any place where the name of God is mentioned. Pride will always remind people about themselves not about others. People will always say, "I am better than so and so. I am the best. People cannot do anything if I am not around. People depend on me. The church cannot prosper without me. Things are always best when I am around."

Ezekiel 28:17 "Your heart became proud on account of your beauty, and you corrupted your wisdom because of your splendour. So I threw you to the earth, I made a spectacle of you before the kings." Pride did not only cause the devil to fall, but it also corrupted his wisdom. That is what normally happens to people. They are blinded because of pride.

Pride and independence from God made Adam and Eve sinners and that prideful nature was passed on the whole race. That is why God hates pride. Even in the New Testament, Paul predicted how the last days would be before our Lord Jesus Christ comes back. **2 Timothy 3:1-5** "But mark this: There will be terrible times in the last days. People will be lovers of themselves, lovers of money, boastful, proud, abusive, disobedient to their parents, ungrateful, unholy, without love, unforgiving, slanderous, without self-control, brutal, not lovers of the good, treacherous, rash, conceited, lovers of pleasure rather than lovers of God – having a form of godliness but denying its power. Having nothing to do with them."

The first item stated in Scripture above is 'lover of themselves.' This is the definition of pride and also on the list boasting and pride are mentioned.

Betty Miller stated that the spiritual beauty is also a deadly trap. **Proverbs 16:18** "Pride goeth before destruction, and a haughty spirit before a fall." God blesses us with His gifts and graces, but then these gifts become a source of pride when we cease to be able to handle them with humbleness. In most cases we began to seeing us as better than others and soon take credit for our holiness and spirituality instead of glorifying God.

We began to refuse to give our gifts back to God because we love to be seen exhibiting them and using them and using them to manipulate, influence, or control others. The Holy Spirit is gentle and likes peace. When this happens, the Holy Spirit will leave us and that is where the Devil will happily replace our gifts with his false gifts. When this happens, the Devil does it in a smooth way that it is not going to be easy for us to realize that our gifts are in the process of being replaced. The difference from this point is that our gifts no longer stress fellowship with God, our gifts do not cause souls to repent, and there is no joy and peace in the Lord. The false gifts will be there to excite the flesh.

The examples of this would be prophecies that promote pride in others, words of knowledge that deal with only the things of this world (houses, cars, lands, business, all luxurious things, etc), or words that promote giving to their ministries. The Bible tells us that we must be careful because even casting out devils and doing wonderful works can be done by those whose hearts are not right with God. "Not everyone who says to me, Lord, Lord, will enter the kingdom of heaven, but only he who does the will of my Father who is in heaven. Many will say to me on that day, Lord, Lord did we not prophecy in your name and in your name drive out demons and perform many miracles? Then I will tell them plainly, I never knew you. Away from me you evildoers; (**Matthew 7:21-23**).

Prayer: *Father, In the name of our Lord and Saviour Jesus Christ, help us to do your will in everything we do. Help us to glorify You with everything we do, and Holy Spirit, do not depart from us, so that we will be able to give our gifts back to our Almighty God for your name to be glorified– Amen.*

According to Alfred H. Ells "Hubris (pride) was the character flaw that caused many to fail in Greek mythology. In his counsel practice, he noticed that it is also the stumbling block for many ministers." **Proverbs 11:2** "When pride comes, then comes disgrace, but with the humble is wisdom." **Proverbs 16:18** "Pride goes before destruction. And a haughty spirit before stumbling." After the Devil realized that he let himself in such destruction, he intended not to be alone in such a situation. He decided to involve Christians in the same situation by striking them with the spirit of pride.

In most instances, pride is probably the major reason for a lack of favour with God and therefore lack of success in ministry.

In the book of Daniel, we read about the king called Nebuchadnezzar who was successful and proud. Nebuchadnezzar was looking down upon the other people. His pride made him not to look up to the sky or to heaven so that he can realize the mercy of the Almighty. He was made to live like animals because of his pride. **Daniel 5:21** "He was driven from people and given the mind of an animal; he lived with the wild donkeys and ate grass like cattle; and his body was drenched with the dew of heaven, until he acknowledge that the Most High God is sovereign over the kingdoms of men and sets over them anyone he wishes." The Bible tells us that he was made to live like an animal until he acknowledged that the Most High God is sovereign, until his pride of looking at himself as the only one above everybody departed from him; only then did Nebuchadnezzar see the mercy of God.

Pride is subtle and can hide in us without our knowledge. Alfred H. Ells stated the signs pride as follows:

Insecurity: Most people feel so insecure that they become provoked if they do not get praise and attention of others. We must understand who we are in Christ to avoid pride. **Proverbs 12:9** "Better to be nobody and yet have a servant than pretend to be somebody and have not food." Insecurity makes us to want to be over others. If we are insecure, we will want ourselves in a superior position because of our inadequacy.

*Dear heavenly Father, help us to accept ourselves as we are, because we were created by you in your image. Help us Father to understand that you have plans with each and every one of us on earth, and we know that when we call on You my Lord, You can hear us because in your Word my Lord You said "For I know the plans I have for you" declares the Lord, plans to give you and not to harm you, plans to give you hope and a future. Then you will call upon me and come and pray to me, and I will listen to you." (**Jeremiah 29:11**) – Amen.*

It is important not to feel insecure and ask God whatever we lack or want in the Name of Jesus Christ, not forgetting to ask in good motive.

The need to be right: People who need to be right think that they know better than others. In most cases they would always say "God told me' or God showed me.' **Galatians 6:3-5** "If anyone thinks he is something when he is nothing, he deceives himself. Each one should test his own actions. Then he can take pride in himself, without comparing himself to somebody else. For each one should carry his own load."

Being argumentative: People who argue their point of view, especially to those in authority over them, are allowing pride to get best of them.

More invested in being heard than hearing: needing to be heard is common among clergy who are insecure. Oftentimes, the individual does not feel loved or valued unless people hear them out. In truth, this is often just an expression of insecurity and pride.

Anger: James 1:20-21 "For the anger of man does not produce the righteousness of God. Therefore, get rid of all moral filth and the evil that is so prevalent and humbly accept the word planted in you, which can save you." An individual who is always angry is suffering from pride. To be on the safe side, choose people whom you can associate with. **Proverbs 22:24** "Do not make friends with a hot-tempered man, do not associate with one easily angered, or you will learn his ways and get yourself ensnared."

Irritability and impatience: Being unable to be patient with others, we become irritated and it demonstrates a haughty view of self. We feel that our views, time, or needs are more important than the other person's. This is more an indication of our pride than someone else's slow movement or imperfection. **Proverbs 15:18** "A hot-tempered man stirs up dissension, but a patient man calms a quarrel." Being patient does not only help us in not being proud, but also in calming the quarrels.

Lack of submissive attitude: Romans 13:5 "Therefore, it is necessary to submit to the authorities, not only because of possible punishment, but also because of conscience." Submission is the voluntary placement of oneself under the influence, control, or authority of another. When an individual pledges their submission to you or another, yet is critical or argumentative of that authority, then pride is the hidden issue. **Hebrews 13:17** "Obey your leaders and submit to their authority…"

Not easily corrected: People who do not accept advice or correction by others have the spirit of pride hiding in them. To be not easily corrected is an element of pride. **Proverbs 13:10** "Pride only breeds quarrels but wisdom is found in those who take advice." Accepting corrections from others shows wisdom. **Proverbs 12:15** "The way of a fool seems right to him, but a wise man listens to advice." "Listen to advice and accept instruction, and in the end you will be wise" **(Proverbs 19:20**).

Receiving correction but not changing: Most people listen to others when they give advice or when correcting them, but there is no change in their lives. They keep on repeating the same mistakes or always do what is not right. Sometimes they listen to you attentively and appear to agree with you or with what you are telling them. This normally happens to people who in their hearts think that they are better than others. If you remain stubborn after many warnings, you will suddenly discover that you have gone too far. "He, that being often reproved hardeneth his neck, shall suddenly be destroyed, and that without remedy" **(Proverbs 29:1).**

Needing others to take your advice: Before you need others to take your advice, first check if you accept advice from others. Many people like to advise others, but they do not take advices from others. This is the element of pride. It is not wrong if people do not accept your advice. It means you have to check and try to motivate your facts and show them how important your advice is. Again, if people do not take your advice, do not be demotivated. They have right to accept it or not. Keep on doing the good job of advising people, especially taking the word of God into the consideration.

Needing to proclaim your title or degrees: There is nothing wrong with titles; but the problem is when one preaches about his/her title all the way. Sometimes people forget to praise God, and they praise themselves about their titles. We must be careful, because too much pride can put us to shame. **Proverbs 11:2** "When pride comes, then comes disgrace, but with the humble is wisdom." Proclaiming our titles sometimes make us to forget that we get everything from God. We forget that God is the provider and our success comes from Him.

Being stubborn: Stubborn people always do not accept admonishing from others. Their word is final and they do not listen to others. They always hurt others and after that they do not feel any remorse or shame. **Proverbs 11:2** "When pride comes, then comes disgrace, but with the humble is wisdom."

Comparing ourselves and competing with others: Comparing and competing is the sign of pride. **2 Corinthians 10:12** "we do not dare to classify or compare ourselves with

32

some who commend themselves. When they measure themselves with themselves, they are wise." Comparing leads to destruction, because we end up comparing or competing with high class people we cannot match. After failing to be like them we end up being sick and stressed. We tend to forget that the grace of God is sufficient for us. **2 Corinthians 12:9** "But He said to me, 'My grace is sufficient for you, for my power is made perfect in weakness." The power of God is made perfect in weaknesses, in sicknesses, in sadness situations, and in everywhere we think we are failing.

There is nothing wrong with wanting to do our best. The problem is when we compare ourselves to others. **Galatians 6:3-5** "If anyone thinks he is something when he is nothing, he deceives himself. Each one should test his own actions. Then he can take pride in himself, without comparing himself to somebody else. For each one should carry his own load." We must compare ourselves to others because if we compare, we will want to be better than others and we would not want to help them. That is where hatred will start.

When Jesus Christ was on earth, He did not forget that He is doing the will of God. He was always humble. When He was on earth He healed many sicknesses and delivered many from bondage, strongholds and soul ties. After helping so many people, there was no sign of pride in him. Instead He would ask people not to tell others what happened to them.

Until pride, which is in us, dies, nothing of heaven can live in us. We must give up ourselves to the meek and humble Holy Spirit. Humbleness must sow the seed, or there can be no reaping in heaven. The same God who humbled Nebuchadnezzar can help us to be humble. God wants our consent. God is able to humble us without our consent, but for us to get the blessing from it that He wants to give us, we are instructed: "Humble yourselves therefore under the mighty hand of God, that he may exalt you in due time" (**1 Peter 5:6**). God is able to do His part, but we must also do our part.

Jesus Christ said in **Matthew 11:28-29** "Come to me, all you who are weary and burdened, and I will give you rest. Take my yoke upon you and learn from me, for I am gentle and humble in heart, and you will find rest for your souls." Pride with its elements can be a burden to us. If we are not aware, we may end up in situations we won't like. Jesus Christ is the Saviour and Redeemer. Making Him our Lord and Saviour in our heart will be a good thing. We must not let pride control us in such a way that we miss the grace of God.

Jesus Christ is our role model. He is God and rich in everything. Because of His humility, He left His glory in heaven and chose to die for us on earth. He was humble on earth and treated us alike. He wanted us to have a balanced self-image, as we were created in his image.

Humbleness, gentleness, and kindness require us to do the following:

We must not compare ourselves with other people or let others compete: Comparing ourselves will make us see ourselves as if we are nothing. If we see ourselves as nothing whereas others are better than us; the spirit of jealousy will be created in us. Jealousy will give birth to hatred and unnecessary anger. Let us discuss anger at a later stage.

We must accept people as they are with their qualities and their weaknesses: if we do not accept people as they are, we are going to have the problem of judging other people. This will lead us to choose people according to their rank or social position, and we will not associate with people of low class/rank.

We must accept ourselves as we are.

We must be happy to see others succeed.

We must recognize our sins, because God need us to be holy and we must be submissive.

Let us check this: Tools for sale

One day the Devil called his agents with the intension of selling his tools. The sale was to be for all the tools discussed above. So, everything was on sale but except two tools, pride and unforgiveness. Then his agents asked him how to go about the sale so they would get good returns. They also questioned him why these two tools (pride and unforgiveness) were not on sale.

Then he said, "I cannot put these two tools on sale, because these are the tools that work for me even if I am nothing else works for me somewhere on this earth. Again you must not forget that one of these tools, pride, is the one that made me fall from heaven. I was thrown out from heaven because of pride. My pride did not allow me to be submissive to God. My pride did not allow me to accept advice from God. My pride did not allow me to receive correction from God. I was argumentative. I did not want to hear anything from God. I compared myself with God, I had the feeling that I am more qualified than God is, I was impatient and I was full of anger.

I was angry because I boasted about my beauty. I knew that I was more beautiful than a star. All these things made me angry and I decided to take the position of God. I wanted to overthrow His kingdom. Then God threw me out from heaven and that is why I am called the prince of this world in **John 12:31**. **Job 41:34** says "......he is king over all that are proud." I am called the king over children of pride.

Now this is the tool that works for me more than any other tool. This is the tool that I use to get Christians where I want them to be. I do not worry about non-believers, because I know for sure that they belong to me. Now with this tool, I catch Christians in such a way that even pastors would say, 'my pride does not allow me to say I am sorry to another pastor.' By this tool, churches break apart. By this tool Christians look down upon the others. By this tool Christian compete and compare themselves to each other. By this tool, children are stubborn towards their parents, pastors and elders of the church. Now there is no way I will put this tool on sale. I know that, however expensive this tool will become, Christians will afford it. This is the tool that works for me."

Now his agents asked again, we can hear you the way you talk about pride that it really works for you. But you also mentioned unforgiveness. What about it? How does it help you, because you said you won't put it on sale just like pride?

He said, "unforgiveness is also as great as pride. The thing is that it also works for me, even if I am not there. I just throw it to the person once, and it multiplies into many tools. When I present the spirit of unforgiveness to the person, I know I am done with that person. Unforgiveness kills both believers and unbelievers. If unforgiveness has to cause sickness, it does so to everyone. People that are unforgiving are struggling from lot of sicknesses. By these sicknesses, they lose faith in God working for them or helping them. They will end up being angry and stating that they do want to hear anything about God.

God does not condemn anybody. God forgives and gives life. Jesus is the way, the truth and life. If we dedicate or re-dedicate our lives to God, He is good and faithful enough to take us back and to remove all our sins which Satan has been holding against us. God forgives and forgets. **Psalm 103:12** "As far as the east is from the west, so far has He removed our transgressions from us."

Let us pray: Father, in the powerful name of our Lord and Saviour Jesus Christ, I thank you for being my Father and me being your Child. I thank you for taking care and watching over me daily. I thank you Lord for giving me another chance of turning back from the way I was living and directing me in the right way. I thank you Lord for giving me the opportunity of recognizing the spirit of pride in me. I surrender myself to you and I pray You to help me to live my life according to the way you want me to live. Help me dear Lord to do everything according to your will. Help me Lord to glorify you in everything I say and everything I do.

I thank my Lord and I believe that you are with me because You said You will never leave us nor forsake us. Lord I thank you for your Word that is a guide to me daily. I thank You Lord in Jesus' Name – Amen.

CHAPTER THREE

UNFORGIVENESS

It is important to understand forgiveness before we get into the issue of unforgiveness as the tool of the Devil. Forgiveness is the willingness to accept and show love toward someone who has wronged us. In this matter we do not count how serious or painful that wrong is. In order word we renounce and completely forget about the wrong. Forgiveness is not just saying the words "I forgive you." What we say must be put in actions. This must come from our hearts and even the person who is forgiven must not find it tough to see this forgiveness.

Forgiveness has benefits that contribute a lot to our daily living. With forgiveness, our fellowship with God flows freely. We must be willing to forgive. Forgiveness also keeps the Devil from getting an advantage over us. **2 Corinthians 2:10-11** "For if you forgive anyone, I also forgive him. And what I have forgiven – if there was anything to forgive – I have forgiven in the sight of Christ for your sake, in order that Satan might not outwit us. For we are not unaware of his schemes." Again we must not let the sun go down on our anger.

Forgiveness comes out in three aspects:

- Forgiving those who did us wrong - who trespass against us - those who made us angry;

- Forgiving ourselves for our past failures (this is the most condemning one if we do not forgive ourselves. It is the same as taking something to destroy ourselves).

- Receiving forgiveness from others against whom we have trespassed.

The issue of unforgiveness was addressed by Jesus when He was teaching his disciples how to pray. **Matthew 6:12** "Forgive us our debts, as we also have forgiven our debtors." Jesus put it clear again that if we forgive others, our heavenly Father will forgive us. "For if you forgive men when they sin against you, your heavenly Father will also forgive you. But if you do not forgive men their sins, your Father will not forgive your sins." (**Matthew 6:14**)

Matthew 5:44-48 " but I say unto you, love your enemies, and pray for them that persecute you; that ye may be sons of your Father who is in heaven: for he maketh his sun to rise on the evil and the good, and sendeth rain on the just and the unjust. For if ye love them that love you, what reward have ye? do not even the publicans the same? And if ye salute your brethren only, what do ye more than others? do not even the Gentiles the same? Ye therefore shall be perfect, as your heavenly Father is perfect.

Unforgiveness is a proof of lack of genuine love in our hearts. Love always protects, Love always trusts, love always hopes and always perseveres (**1 Corinthians 13:7**).

Unforgiveness make us not to prosper because we hold on to the past. We do not want to practice what our heavenly is doing. We expect our God to treat us the way we do not want to treat others. Paul stated that we must "Forgive each other, just as God in Christ has also forgiven you" (**Ephesians 4:32**). Unforgiveness is the evil spirit that torments.

We must not fool ourselves that we can live with unforgiveness and get away with it because it will kill us. God sent his Son to help us because he loved us. Jesus Christ was not only sent for forgiveness; He was also sent to cleanse us completely, so that unforgiveness has no effect on us anymore. **1 John 1:9** "If we confess our sins, He is faithful and just to forgive us our sins, and to cleanse us from all unrighteousness."

Paul advises us in **Ephesians 4:31-32** to "Get rid of all bitterness. rage and anger, brawling and slander, along with every form of malice. Be kind and compassionate to one another, forgiving each other, just as in Christ God forgave you." Paul was mentioning these as he knew that they are under the umbrella of unforgiveness.

Many people are controlled by the spirit of unforgiveness, and that is where the sicknesses lie. The unforgiving heart causes problems in life. Unforgiving heart is full of hatred. Hatred causes us to be impatient. Impatience make us unhappy with many things and an unhappy heart causes us not to respond to medicine. **Proverbs 17-22** "A cheerful heart is good medicine, but a crushed spirit dries up the bones." When our bones are dry, we are just like dead people.

Unforgiveness is something that can really hold us back from escaping the corruption of sin and living for God. Unforgiveness actually block God's forgiveness of our sin and provides a foothold for the devil to influence our lives.

Unforgiveness has some consequences that disturb Christians in their life of fellowship with God peacefully. In **Mark 11:25** we read "And whenever you stand praying, if you have anything against anyone, forgive him in that your Father who is in heaven may also forgive you, your own failings and shortcomings, but if you do not forgive, neither will your Father in heaven forgive your failings and shortcomings."

Unforgiveness hinders prayers

Matthew 6:14-15 "For if you forgive men when they sin against you, your heavenly Father will also forgive you. But if you do not forgive men their sins, your Father will not forgive your sins." If we are praying for God to forgive our sins and we do not forgive others their sins, the Bible says God, our Father will not forgive us. This means our prayer for forgiveness is hindered by our unforgiveness.

Unforgiveness stands in the way of Christians to get their healing, to get their peace with God and everyone on earth, it blocks their blessings and prosperity and problems remain unsolved. Parents who are broken up and who cannot forgive each other, make their children suffer consequences of their hard hearts and unfogiveness. Divorce hurts children and leaves them to be attacked by anger. Angry children become problematic in the society. Unforgiveness of the parents may lead to unforgiving children. Parents must think otherwise before they get into this action.

As parents we need to forgive our children no matter what they do at whatever age. If we do not; we lead them to be rebellious, and this will cause them to not honour us as their parents. If we punish them, we must punish them with love, showing them that we love them and we want the best for them.

Ephesians 6:1-3 "Children, obey your parents in the Lord, for this is right. Honour your father and mother – which is the first commandment with a promise that it may go well with you and that you may enjoy life on the earth." This commandment was written first in the book of **Exodus 20:12** in the Old Testament. Children must not provoke their parents and lead them to unforgiveness. Children must be careful of whom they associate with. The association may lead to other things that are contrary to what our parents like. There is no parent who will like it when his/her child gets involved in drugs, alcohol use, violence or witchcraft. God is against all these things. Whatever God does not like, our parents will also not like.

Parents are protective to their children. Whatever they do, they are trying to protect them. Children must forgive them so that their prayers are not hindered when they pray.

Our sins which are not confessed and cleansed hinder our communication with God. These sins grieve our Helper, the Holy Spirit. We must daily confess our sins and ask for forgiveness. **Ephesians 4:32** tells us to "Be kind and compassionate to one another, forgiving each other, just as in Christ God forgave you."

God did not want our prayers to be hindered. Hence it was stated in **Matthew 18:21-22** "Then Peter came to Jesus and asked, Lord, how many times shall I forgive my brother when he sins against me? Up to seven time? Jesus answered, 'I tell you, not seven times, but seventy-seven times."

We cannot walk with God while harbouring unforgiveness in our hearts, because we would not agree with Him. Our Heavenly Father is a forgiving God. When we walk with Him it means we are walking in forgiveness. If we are not prepared to forgive, it means we are not free from faults. That means we will not ask anything from our Father. Our Lord is commanding us to forgive the debts of others .

Jesus prayed for His disciples and for us. His prayers were not hindered, because the spirit of forgiveness was in Him. **Luke 22:63-65** "The men who were guarding Jesus began mocking and beating him. They blindfolded him and demanded, 'Prophesy! Who hit you?" And they said many other insulting things to him." But He did hold grudge on them.

If we check this Scripture: **Matthew 27:27- 44** "Some of the governor's soldiers took Jesus into their headquarters and called out the entire regiment. They stripped him and put a scarlet robe on him. They wove thorn branches into a crown and put it on his head, and they placed a reed stick in his right hand as a sceptre. Then they knelt before him in mockery and taunted, "Hail! King of the Jews!" And they spit on him and grabbed the stick and struck him on the head with it. When they were finally tired of mocking him, they took off the robe and put his own clothes on him again. Then they led him away to be crucified.

Along the way, they came across a man named Simon, who was from Cymene, and the soldiers forced him to carry Jesus' cross. And they went out to a place called Golgotha (which means "Place of the Skull"). The soldiers gave him wine mixed with bitter gall, but when he had tasted it, he refused to drink it.

After they had nailed him to the cross, the soldiers gambled for his clothes by throwing dice. Then they sat around and kept guard as he hung there. A sign was fastened to the cross above Jesus' head, announcing the charge against him. It read: "This is Jesus, the King of the Jews." Two revolutionaries were crucified with him, one on his right and one on his left.

The people passing by shouted abuse, shaking their heads in mockery. "Look at you now!" they yelled at him. "You said you were going to destroy the Temple and rebuild it in three days. Well then, if you are the Son of God, save yourself and come down from the cross!"

The leading priests, the teachers of religious law, and the elders also mocked Jesus. "He saved others," they scoffed, "but he can't save himself! So he is the King of Israel, is he? Let him come down from the cross right now, and we will believe in him! He trusted God, so let God rescue him now if he wants him! For he said, 'I am the Son of God.'" Even the revolutionaries who were crucified with him ridiculed him in the same way."

But on top of all these this things, Jesus still loved them and asked the Lord to forgive them. They whipped him. They did not know that those whip marks were to our advantage because we are healed. They put a scarlet robe on him. Luke and John mentioned that they put purple robes on him, like the robe worn by a king. This because they were mocking him. The colour for scarlet symbolized the blood of the lamb which was going to be shed for us. They did not know that He was the actual crown prince of the greater Israel nation, but also our King of kings and Prince of princes. They put a crown of thorns on his head as also a mockery to laugh at Him. The spat on Him, but in all those things he forgave them and asked God to forgive them **Luke 23:34** "Jesus said, 'Father, forgive them, for they do not know what they are doing."

Jesus was praying this prayer because He did not want their prayers to be hindered. He knew that one day they will request some of the things from God. **Psalm 24:1** "The earth in the Lord's and everything in it, the world and all who live in it."

"If we have sin hidden in our hearts, we cannot pray with confidence that God will answer. However, if we ask Him to reveal those hidden sins, He will. (Joyce Mayer: 2007). Unforgiveness is a sin that can hide in our hearts. **Psalm 66:18** "If I regard inequity in my heart, the Lord will not hear me." This simply means if we hold unforgiveness in our hearts, God will not hear us when we pray, and will not answer us when we pray. Our God loves us so much that He promised us power and sound mind, free from fear.   **2 Timothy 1:7** "For God did not give us the spirit of timidity, but a spirit of power, of love and of self-discipline." God wants us to love our neighbours, even if they make life difficult for us. He must forgive them so that we do not hold back the answers to our prayers.

UNFORGIVENESS DESTROYS RELATIONSHIPS

1. Unforgiveness is like a wall. When builders start to build, we cannot see the progress for the first two or three days. After few days the wall is thick, high and strong. When a wall is this high and strong, it is not

easy to break. A wall is a boundary between us and our beloved ones. It will take days for one to break this wall completely. Unforgiveness works like that. If we want to break the wall of unforgiveness, we have to take some days. These will be days of seeking the face of God, fellowshipping with God, and asking Him to cleanse us. The closer we become to God, the better we will know Him and the better we can deal with unforgiveness, because the Lord himself commanded us to forgive.

2. Unforgiveness produces bitterness. Bitter people do not love others. They do not want to associate with other people. They want to be alone. To be alone is just like not wanting to be with God. Unforgiveness makes people not want to fellowship with God. People who are bitter are just like people who are carrying heavy loads on their shoulders. For these people to be freed from this load, Jesus Christ is the answer.

3. Unforgiving parents destroy their children: Children who grow in the environment of unforgiving parents also become unforgiving as they grow up. They adopt this spirit because they think it is the right thing to do. Parents must be careful about how they raise their children. Children must be raised in the environment where the love of God is the foundation in the house.

4. Unforgiveness makes us deceive ourselves by thinking that we control the situations. Some people think that when they do not forgive others it is a sign that they understand their rights. They think they know how and where to put others. They think that if you do not forgive someone it means you are showing him that you are not manipulated.

The number one stumbling block in marriages is unforgiveness. Couples think that if you forgive somebody his/her faults, it means that you are stupid. Jesus Christ died on the cross for all of us to be forgiven so that we will also forgive others. We cannot expect Christ to forgive us if we do not want to forgive others.

God loves us and forgives us, no matter what we do. We must love and forgive others just as our Lord does. We must practice daily what our Father does to us, forgiving, loving and accepting others with their faults. That is what God is doing to us.

Many Christians are living defeated lives because they are hanging onto their pasts. They see their sins more than they see the solution to their sins, and that is the blood of Jesus Christ. People spent more of their time dwelling in their sins than on what Jesus has done for them.

Unforgiveness is not changed by time. We must take action in order to forgive and to be forgiven. There is only one cure for unforgiveness, namely to forgive and forget. It is important to understand the two. One cannot forget and get healed without forgiving, but one can get healed by forgiving plus forgetting. Forgetting cannot take the sickness away, but forgiving does. So in this we can say one can even forgive and get healed without forgetting. Let us forgive and forget, then.

We must allow the Holy Spirit to take control and to remove obstacles for us. We cannot do that on our own. In most instances people get saved, but do not repent from not responding to forgiveness. When forgiveness calls, people will remember mistakes and past failures of others and will start counting on them. They get stuck on that and refuse to forgive others. We must not allow our condition to hold the Holy Spirit back.

Unforgiveness is a sin, so if we let it go, confess it, and repent, we can have an immense feeling of relief and peace. Everything can change by just saying the simple words; "I forgive you." It is not wrong to add spice on it by saying "I love you." There must be love in forgiveness. Forgiving is not an emotion, but an action. We born-again Christians have the strength from God to be able to forgive. This strength was given to us because it is required in our relationship with Him.

52

Jesus Christ died for us to enjoy forgiveness, because He led by example by forgiving us our debts, and lastly He forgave those who persecuted him by saying "Father forgive them because they do not know what they are doing." They did not know that they were already forgiven.

Sometimes it hurts to find out that you are holding onto something that has been released for you a long time ago. The Lord Jesus Christ forgave us all. Now it is for us to forgive each other, and not to hold anything against each other.

Let us release to Lord Jesus Christ those pains and those people who wronged us, because He called everybody who is heavy laden. **Matthew 11:28-29** "Come to me, all you who are weary and burdened, and I will give you rest. Take my yoke upon you and learn from me, for I am gentle and humble in heart, and you will find rest for your souls."

There is no sin that is too great for God to forgive. **Isaiah 1:18** "Come now, let us reason together, says the Lord. Though you sins are like scarlet, they shall be like wool." God forgives all sins. The sin that God cannot forgive is the one that is not taken to Him.

Holy Spirit wants to minister love, joy, and peace in us. By the power of the Holy Spirit, the tools of the Devil are nothing. We must outstretch our arm as a sign of forgiveness. The father of the lost son threw his arms around the neck of his son. **Luke 15:20** "....But while he was a long way off, his father saw him and was filled with compassion for him; he ran to his son, threw his arms around him and kissed him."

There is no condemnation in Christ. **Romans 8:1** "Therefore there is no condemnation for those who are in Christ Jesus." Jesus came to save us and to remove our past from our new lives.

The Lord forgives. That is why He wants us to forgive others. God was prepared to forgive Cain for his anger, because He advised him about the sin that is crouching at his door. This means God was giving Cain a chance to repent.

Jesus Christ knew the danger of unforgiveness and the damage that it can cause if people do not forgive each other. Jesus Christ taught us to forgive each other seventy times seven. "Then Peter came to Jesus and asked, Lord, how many times shall I forgive my brother when he sins against me? Up to seven time? Jesus answered, 'I tell you, not seven times, but seventy-seven times'" (**Matthew 18:21-22**).

70 x7 equals 490. This is the number for spiritual perfection. The number seven (7) is God's number for perfection, ten (10) stands for completion. (In calculations, 7X7X10=490.) That is Spiritual perfection. If we really want Spiritual perfection, we

would not have hard feeling for others, we would not hold grudges, we will do away with bitterness and anger then we will be in peace with others and God our Father will be with us forever.

When I was still young working in the industries before I joined an academic institution, we used to buy everything that was sold. Clothes, cutlery, dishes, and anything you can think of. People who sold these things were giving us opportunity to pay as we go or as we use them. Everybody would sell whatever he/she liked.

You would find that the one who is selling clothes will also buy something from someone who sells something else. Not everybody would pay cash. We used to pay in instalments. Even if one could pay cash, we were used to this type of payment and we were comfortable with it.

One day, one lady went to the one who owed her the money for the shoes and requested payment. The lady who bought shoes did not have money and she asked for forgiveness so that she could pay the next week. The owner of the shoes understood and forgave her that she could not pay her. And they had to part.

Immediately the lady, who was forgiven, saw the one who owed her the money for dishes. She suddenly grabbed her and requested her money. That lady also did not have money. She asked for forgiveness and requested to be given a chance of paying her debt the following week. The owner of the dishes did not understand and she was shouting this poor lady.

Fortunately, one lady who was present when the one who owe the money for the shoes was forgiven came and said to her "you are no good. You did not pay the owner of shoes and she forgave you but you cannot forgive this poor lady because she cannot pay you the money for the dishes. You must think otherwise. You are forgiven, now you must also forgive others. Just as that lady forgave you, you must also forgive this one."

She could not understand, but at the end she had to, because that lady threatened that if she did not forgive the one who owed her the money for the dishes, she would call the lady of the shoes and tell her the whole story. And that is how the poor lady was rescued.

I looked at them and this reminds of what Jesus told his disciples in:

Matthew 18:23-35 "Therefore is the kingdom of heaven likened unto a certain king, who would make a reckoning with his servants. And when he had begun to reckon, one was brought unto him that owed him ten thousand talents. But forasmuch as he had not wherewith to pay, his lord commanded him to be sold, and his wife, and children, and all that he had, and payment to be made.

The servant therefore fell down and worshipped him, saying, Lord, have patience with me, and I will pay thee all. And the lord of that servant, being moved with compassion, released him, and forgave him the debt. But that servant went out, and found one of his fellow-servants, who owed him a hundred shillings: and he laid hold on him, and took him by the throat, saying, Pay what thou owest. So his fellow-servant fell down and besought him, saying, Have patience with me, and I will pay thee. And he would not: but went and cast him into prison, till he should pay that which was due. So when his fellow-servants saw what was done, they were exceeding sorry, and came and told unto their lord all that was done.

Then his lord called him unto him, and saith to him, Thou wicked servant, I forgave thee all that debt, because thou be soughtest me: shouldest not thou also have had mercy on thy fellow-servant, even as I had mercy on thee? And his lord was wroth, and delivered him to the tormentors, till he should pay all that was due. So shall also my heavenly Father do unto you, if ye forgive not everyone his brother from your hearts. "

Unforgiveness is one of the most popular poisons that the enemy uses against God's people, and it is one of the deadliest poisons a person can take spiritually. Unforgiveness can harm our physical health. It causes everything from mental depression to health problems such as cancer and arthritis. One wise man once said "unforgiveness is the act of drinking poison and hoping someone else dies." A person who holds onto unforgiveness, is not aware that he is killing himself. He always thinks that by not forgiving someone he is killing that person, only to find that he is killing himself. Jesus Christ spoke many times about unforgiveness, because He did not want us to be caught up in sickness and not being free.

Unforgiveness shows that we hate Jesus: If we do not forgive, it means we are not like our Lord Jesus Christ. If we do not act like him, it means we do not love him. We cannot say we love Jesus Christ if we oppose what He wants us to do.

Most bad relationships are a result of vanity, strife, or envy. Many times, strife starts off with a simple tease, but then turns into a slap or insult. We need to show love and forgiveness, as God loved us first and has forgiven us. Lying and keeping secrets from one another are causes for and relationship. Bad relationships make us not to love Jesus Christ. Loving others that do not love us is true Christian ministry that brings us and others closer to God.

In **John 15:12**, Jesus commands us to love one another, as He has loved us. True love doesn't hold bitterness or unforgiveness against that person. If we are bitter or hold unforgiveness against somebody, then we do not love them as Christ loved us. If we do not keep Jesus' commandment, then it proves that we do not love Him. **John 14:24** "He who does not love me will not obey my teaching."

Unforgiveness is a wall that blocks God from forgiving us: "But if you forgive not men their debts, neither will your Father forgive you your debts" (**Matthew 6:15**). To forgive others for their debts is not an easy thing but because we live under the law of our Father, we have to forgive them. God knew how he is going to help us when He made this command. God will not command us to do something that He knows we cannot carry out. We must not let unforgiveness prevent God from forgiving us. God is willing to forgive us and our duty is to also forgive others.

Unforgiveness opens us up to the tormentors: The devil is greatest tormentor in the world. He will deceive us by showing us that there is no need for forgiveness. He can also show us how better off we are without forgiveness, but he will never show us the consequences of unforgiveness. Unforgiveness can torment us with diseases such as depression, stress, cancer and others.

Unforgiveness can corrupt a person: If there is a sin that defiles/corrupts a person, then unforgiveness is that sin. It can corrupt the life of a person who in turn defiles the earth by not obeying the laws and by violating the statutes. Isaiah24:5 "The earth is defiled by its people; they have disobeyed the laws, violated the statutes, and broken the everlasting covenant."

Unforgiveness is another loophole that devil uses to get people: At all the times the devil is looking for a loophole where he can enter into our lives. Not forgiving other people makes it easy for him to torment us.

Unforgiveness is another way to hell: Sometimes people categorize sins. They think some sins are less important and one can live with them and still go to heaven. People think that they can do everything that our Lord wants us to do but live their lives without forgiving others. They forget the words of our Lord "Forgive us our debts and we forgive others their debts." People are so familiar with this phrase that I think sometimes they do not hear what they are saying. It is just like a song that can be sung without the singer realizing or understanding what the song says.

Unforgiveness causes spiritual death: It hinders us from reaching the high calling of God in our life. It can hinder our Spiritual walk with God. Paul warned us against refusing God. "See to it that no one misses the grace of God, and that no bitterroot grows up to cause trouble and defile many" (**Hebrews 12:15**).

Curses come through unforgiveness: Some of the curses we experience do not need highly spiritual solutions. It is simply a matter of forgiveness.

We must be like David. Although he committed many sins, he was called "a man next to the heart of God" because he was not stubborn to repent. He had a repentant heart. One of his psalms acknowledging his sins is **Psalm 51:3-4** "For I know my transgressions, and my sin is always before me. Against You, only You, have I sinned and done what is evil in your sight, so that you are proved right when you speak." Although David committed many sins, he wanted to stand before God clean and made whole.

The word of God tells us that everything, good or bad, is for the good of those who love the Lord. **Romans 8:28** "And we know that in all things (good or bad) God works for the good of those who love him, who have been called according to his purpose."

Joseph was sold as a slave by his brothers, and suffered for many years in Egypt, but he forgave them and accepted them after he became viceroy in Egypt. **Genesis 37:18** "....So Joseph went after his brothers and found them near Dothan. But they saw him in the distance, and before he reached them, they plotted to kill him." First of all, his brothers were **angry** that he thinks he can rule them. The **anger** in them led to unforgiveness. Unforgiveness led to hatred that will lead to murder. Fortunately they did not kill him but they sold him.

They thought they had solved the problem by removing him before their eyes. They did not know that it was the plan of God that would work for their good in future. Again Joseph was put in jail by the wife of his master by telling he husband lies about Joseph. **Genesis 39:16**- "She kept his cloak beside her until his master came home: 'The Hebrew slave you brought us came to me to make sport of me. But as soon as I screamed for help, he left his cloak beside me and ran out of the house. When his master heard the story his wife told him, saying, 'This is how your slave treated me, he burned with **anger**. Joseph's master took him and put him in prison, the place where the king's prisoners were confined."

On top of all these things, Joseph did not hold any grudge against anybody. He forgave his brothers and received them in Egypt during the famine that struck their land. **Genesis 45:4-5** "Then Joseph said to his brothers 'come close to me.' When they had done so, he said, I am your brother Joseph, the one you had sold into Egypt! And now, do not be distressed and do not be **angry** with yourselves for selling me here, because it was to save lives that God sent me ahead of you."

Forgiveness is easy if we can swallow our pride and forgive first before we expect to be forgiven. God wants us to live our lives abundantly because He set us free and we must be free in deed.

Jesus Christ must be our role model. He forgave those who crucified him with criminals. **Luke 23:33-34** "When they came to the place called the Skull, there they crucified him, along with the criminals- one on his right, the other on his left. Jesus said, 'Father; forgive them, for they do not know what they are doing."

If we do not pray or forgive others, we are prisoners and we are not aware. If we forgive others, we set prisoners free ,that means we set ourselves free.

Remedy: "Forgive and live in harmony with others. Read the Word of God and meditate on it. Love others as you love yourself. See yourself as a forgiven saint not a forgiven sinner. Take this medicine on daily basis and you will be permanently healed."

Let us pray: Dear heavenly Father, thank you for making me aware of this sin of unforgiveness. Help to forgive the debts of others as I know that when I request you to forgive me, you will forgive as your Word promises: "forgive us our debts as we forgive others their debts." I repent from this sin of unforgiveness right now, and I rededicate my life to you in Jesus' Name. I would like to believe in my heart and to confess with my mouth that you are our Lord and You died for us on the Cross for all our sins to be forgiven. Help me dear Father not to hinder my prayers because of unforgiveness. Help me to accept and love people as they are, because they were are also created by You in your image. I am asking this in Jesus' Name – Amen.

CHAPTER FOUR

THE ELEMENTS OF UNFORGIVENESS

Bitterness, anger and hatred are the elements of unforgiveness. We must get rid of them so that we can live better lives in fellowship with our God.

Bitterness:

We must understand that bitter root in our lives produces bitter fruit until everything we think or do seems wrong. **Ephesians 12:15** "See to it that no one misses the grace of God, and that no bitter root grows up to cause trouble and defile many."

Many authors have a different explanation for bitterness but the fact is they are all explanations for bitterness. Bitterness can be seen or realized from person's actions and expressions. If one has drunk a bitter drink, you will see from the facial expression that something is not right with the person. This also applies to bitterness inside us; our actions will show others we are bitter, even if we do not say it in words.

After checking different sources, the following explanation was taken from www.charminghealth.com. "Bitterness is a frozen form of latent anger and resentment. Bitterness grows out of our refusal, to let go when someone or something is taken

65

from us. It is constantly hurt by a memory and holding onto it until it has a hold on you."

When it is mentioned that bitterness is a fruit of unforgiveness, it means that unforgiveness is produced by bitterness, anger, and wrath. Bitterness is caused by hurtful words, hurtful attitudes and hurtful actions directed against us by from others. When we are offended by others, we must not allow this to germinate in our hearts so that bitterness will take root.

We must be aware, because bitterness can make us idiots. Bitterness makes people short-tempered and they end up doing stupid things. From the stupid things we do, we end up being hurt. This can lead to suicidal feelings. Bitterness is regarded a slow poison, because with bitterness in our hearts, our daily lives will be miserable.

Bitterness must be avoided as much as possible. If we do not avoid bitterness, our relationship with God will be damaged. This relationship is damaged because if things are not going well in life, we often end up blaming God. We forget that God is the source everything we need in life. God has never made a promise that He did not keep. **Isaiah 41:9-10** "I took you from the ends of the earth; from its farthest corners I called you. I said, 'You are my servant': I have chosen you and have not rejected you. So do not fear, for I am with you; do not be dismayed, for I am your God."

We must avoid listening to the Devil who always tells us that God has forgotten us or we are not good enough to be His children. God is our Father there is no way He can leave us nor forsake us. **Joshua 1:5** "....so I will be with you; I will never leave you nor forsake you." This is a promise from God and He always keeps his promises.

Unforgiveness is like a poison that can kill someone. Being free from bitterness is like a medicine that can fight the poison. The poison we drank need to be diluted. The first step is to go to our Father, the creator of everything, and ask Him to take control of our lives.

God will not operate with a Spirit of unforgiveness. He will not operate with bitterness. Jesus Christ told his disciples the parable of the lost son. Jesus Christ here was trying to show them that our father does not operate with a spirit of unforgiveness. **Luke 15:11-31:** "To further illustrate this point, Jesus told them this story: "A man had two sons. The younger son told his father, 'I want my share of your estate now before you die.' So his father agreed to divide his wealth between his sons. "A few days later, this younger son packed all his belongings and moved to a distant land, and there he wasted all his money in wild living. About the time his money ran out, a great famine swept over the land, and he began to starve. He persuaded a local farmer to hire him, and the man sent him to feed the pigs. The young man became so hungry that even the pods he was feeding the pigs looked good to him. But no one gave him anything.

"When he finally came to his senses, he said to himself, 'At home even the hired servants have food enough to spare, and here I am dying of hunger! I will go home to my father and say, "Father, I have sinned against both heaven and you, and I am no longer worthy of being called your son. Please take me on as a hired servant."'" There must be a time where we come to our senses and go back to our Father (God) and tell Him that we have sinned and that we want to repent from whatever evil things we did.

"So he returned home to his father. And while he was still a long way off, his father saw him coming. Filled with love and compassion, he ran to his son, embraced him, and kissed him. His son said to him, 'Father, I have sinned against both heaven and you, and I am no longer worthy of being called your son.'" There is one thing we must know, our Father is waiting for us to come back and ask for forgiveness.

"But his father said to the servants, 'Quick! Bring the finest robe in the house and put it on him. Get a ring for his finger and sandals for his feet. And kill the calf we have been fattening. We must celebrate with a feast, ^{for} this son of mine was dead and has now returned to life. He was lost, but now he is found.' So the party began.

"Meanwhile, the older son was in the fields working. When he returned home, he heard music and dancing in the house, and he asked one of the servants what was going on. 'Your brother is back,' he was told, 'and your father has killed the fattened calf. We are celebrating because of his safe return.'

"The older brother was angry and wouldn't go in. His father came out and begged him, but he replied, 'All these years I've slaved for you and never once refused to do a single thing you told me to. And in all that time you never gave me even one young goat for a feast with my friends. Yet when this son of yours comes back after squandering your money on prostitutes, you celebrate by killing the fattened calf!'

"His father said to him, 'Look, dear son, you have always stayed by me, and everything I have is yours. But we had to celebrate and be glad, because this brother of yours was dead and is alive; he was lost and is found.'" Sometimes we miss the point that everything that belongs to our Father is ours too.

The lost son knew that his father would forgive him because his father did not have an unforgiving spirit. We must be like our Father. The lost son knew that his father would never forsake him. Even if he is the one who left his father, his father will never leave him, nor forsake him. Even if we leave our father and concentrate on the things of the world, our Father will always be there, waiting to accept us back. The lost son knew that in his father's house there is everything. "The earth is of the lord and everything in it" (**Psalm 24:1**).

The lost son acknowledged that he had sinned against his father and heaven. **Verse 21** "The son said to him, 'father, I have sinned against heaven and against you ...'"
Unforgiveness is a sin and we must acknowledge this sin.

Jesus Christ compared unforgiveness with a **Sycamine** tree (Mulberry tree). **Luke 17:6** (KJM) "And the Lord said, If ye had faith as a grain of mustard seed, ye might say unto this sycamine tree, Be thou plucked up by the root, and be thou planted in the sea; and it should obey you." In INV translations "if you have faith as small as a mustard seed, you can say to this **Mulberry** tree, 'Be uprooted and planted in the sea, and it will obey you."

From WikiAnswers.com "The Sycamine tree and mulberry tree were very similar in appearance; the two trees even produced a fruit that looked identical. However, the fruit of the Sycamine tree was extremely bitter. Its fruit looked just as luscious and delicious as a mulberry fig but when a person tasted the Sycamine fig, he discovered that it was horribly bitter.

Mulberry figs were delicious and therefore expensive. Because of the cost of this fruit, it was primarily eaten by wealthier people. But the Sycamine fig was cheap and therefore affordable to the poorer people. Because the poor couldn't afford the luscious mulberry fig, they munched on the Sycamine fig as a substitute (Answers.com).

The sycamine tree has the following characteristics which will make one understand why Jesus used this tree:

-   **The sycamine tree had a very large and deep root structure:** In the Middle East, this tree was known to have one of the deepest root structures of all trees. Its roots grew down deep into the earth and it was difficult to kill. Hot weather and blistering temperatures had little effect on this tree, because it was usually tapped into a water source down deep under the earth. Because of its deepest roots under the ground, it was not easy for it to be killed even if one can cut its base. These deep roots would draw from the underground sources of water, enabling it to keep resurfacing again and again.

71

Bitterness and unforgiveness were compared to this tree. To kill this tree altogether, the roots must be dealt with thoroughly and this is how bitterness and unforgiveness must be dealt with. They must be taken out from their roots. Their roots go down deep into the human soul, fed by any offence that lies hidden in the soil of the heart.

For the person with the spirits of bitterness and unforgiveness to be set free, it will take a serious decision for that person to rip those roots off so that they do not grow again. The person must turn to God completely.

- **The Sycamine tree's wood was the preferred wood for building caskets:** This is because it would grow quickly and would be accessible in many different places. That is why it is compared with bitterness and unforgiveness because they can also grow quickly ruin the relationships with other people because of the ugly attitude and fast growth.

As sycamine grows easily in dry places, so does bitterness in dry spiritual conditions. Where there is no joy, no peace, no repentance and no love, that is where bitterness and unforgiveness enjoy tormenting us. Bitterness and unforgiveness can take us six-feet underground quickly, just like sycamine wood caskets and coffins.

Rick Renner stressed this "If you permit bitterness and unforgiveness to grow in your life, it won't be long until these attitudes have killed your joy, stolen your peace, and cancelled out your spiritual life!"

- **The sycamine tree produced a fig that was very bitter to eat**: The sycamine tree fruits looked identical to mulberry fruits. The difference is that sycamine fruits looked delicious and luscious but they are extremely bitter whereas mulberry fruits are delicious and expensive. The fruit for bitterness and unforgiveness are cheap and bitter and this bitterness can lead us to death.

Bitterness and unforgiveness may grow deeper in that manner but the good news is that Jesus is the healer of all sickness. Jesus Christ set us free from all bondages. It is the matter of deciding to get healed. Jesus Christ wants us to have that joy, peace and happiness again.

Let us pray: Dear heavenly Father, I thank you for talking to me and showing me the death penalty I am facing with this bitterness and unforgiveness. I ask you, my Lord, to set me free right now in the Name of Jesus Christ who died for us on the cross. Lord, I asking this because it is written in Isaiah 53:5 "But He was pierced for our transgressions, He was crushed for our iniquities; the punishment that brought us peace was upon him, and by his wounds we are healed." I confess that I have not forgiven as you have commanded us to. In the name of Jesus Christ I now forgive these people:_____ (list the names of those people). Please forgive and cleanse my sin and I want to be pure and walk in your ways now. Help me to do everything according to you will. I am asking you to heal my wounds and I thank you in Jesus' Name - Amen

We must thank God for all things that happened and for those we have received from God. The Bible tells us in **1 Thessalonians 5:18** "Give thanks in all circumstances, for this is God's will for you in Christ Jesus." Everything that happens to us is of the good course from God. We must stop blaming God for whatever things happened to us. We must start praying God to forgive us for blaming Him for what we thought about our Lord which is not good.

Let us pray: Dear heavenly Father, I recognize my sin of unforgiveness toward you regarding :_____(mention the situation). I know that you are perfectly just and holy, although I may not understand why things happened as they did. Lord please help me to forgive You for my offence and everything I said which is not good about You. I confess with my mouth that I love you Lord and I know that you died for me on the cross for me to get healed and to have joy, peace and love. I ask all these in Jesus' Name – Amen.

Anger

Ephesians 4:26-27 "In your anger, do not sin. Do not let the sun go down while you are still angry, and do not give a devil a foothold." We must remember that the Devil must have a foothold before he can get a stronghold. Let us not help him to torture us. Forgiveness is the quick answer. (Joyce Meyer)

Unforgiveness is not new in this era. It started in the Garden of Eden when Cain was unable to forgive his brother Abel because of the differentiation in the sacrifice. Abel's sacrifice was accepted by God, and this made Cain angry until he killed his brother. **Genesis 4:4-8** "….The Lord looked with favour on Abel and his offering, but on Cain and his offering he did not look with favour. So Cain was **angry**, and his face was downcast. Then the Lord said to Cain, 'why are you angry? Why is your face downcast? If you do what is right, will you not be accepted? But if you do not do what is right, sin is crouching at your door; it desires to have you, but you must master it.' Now Cain said to his brother Abel, 'Let's go out to the field.' And while they were in the field, Cain attacked his brother Abel and killed him."

We must be like our God who is slow to anger. **Exodus 34:6** ".....The Lord is compassionate and gracious God, slow to anger, abounding love to thousands, and faithfulness." A person who is slow to anger normally has compassion and love for others. In most cases, things are destroyed because people are angry.

We must not be harsh in words when we talk to others. **Proverbs 15:1** "A gentle answer turns away wrath but a harsh word stirs up anger." We must be like our Lord, for He is gentle and humble. Humble people always like peace and harmony. **Matthew 11:29** "Take my yoke upon you and learn from me, for I am gentle in heart, and you will find rest for you souls."

Anger is a spirit. The Bible warns us not to associate with those who are easily angered. **Proverbs 22:24** "Do not make friends with a hot tempered man, do not associate with one easily angered, or you may learn his ways and get yourself ensnared." Christians must teach their children how to behave and the people they associate with. Easily angered people are no good. We must pray for them to be like our Lord.

Lastly in **James 1:19,** the Bible teaches us this "Everyone should be quick to listen, slow to speak and slow to become angry, for man's anger does not bring about the righteous life that God desires. Therefore get rid of all moral filth and the evil that is so prevalent and humbly accept the word planted in you, which can save you."

Hatred

"Hatred or hate is a word that describes intense feelings of dislike" (Dr. Syed Shahid). **Proverbs 10:12** "Hatred stirs up dissension but love covers all wrongs." As Christians, we must have the love of Jesus Christ that will cover the wrongs for our fellow brothers. It was because of love that our Lord Jesus Christ died on the cross.

Ephesians 4:31 "Get rid of all bitterness, rage and anger, brawling and slander, along with every form of malice. Be kind and compassionate to one another, forgiving each other, just as a Christ God forgave you." If we get rid of hatred and anger in us, we will be able to forgive other without holding on the past.

*Let us pray: Dear heavenly Father, help me to get rid of anger in my soul. I know You love me and I know my identity in you. Your Word in **Ezekiel 38:26** says "I will give you a new heart and put a new spirit in you. I will remove from you your heart of stone and give you a heart of flesh. And I will put my spirit in you and move you to follow my decrees and be careful to keep my laws." I give myself to you my Lord to do anything* *with my heart so that I can live in harmony with everybody. I ask these in Jesus' Name, Amen.*

CHAPTER FIVE

BONDAGE

Until we understand what bondage in Christians is, we are not going to be able to understand who we are in Christ. Bondage is caused by ignorance, strongholds and deception. The devil is using ignorance and strongholds to deceive people. It is important for Christians to know who they are in Christ, and that Christ is in them and for them.

Understanding and knowing the picture of God in us is one of the best weapons that we can use to conquer the enemy. If we do not see God as our Father who is always with us to protect us during times of trouble , we will fall into in the trap of the enemy every time. **Joshua 1:5** "No one will be able to stand up against you all the days of your life. As I was with Moses, so I will never leave you nor forsake you."

Our relationship with God is of value and our Lord does not want to lose us. That is why He sends His only Son to die for us so we can have everlasting life. Lack of knowledge is death.

If we view ourselves as nothing and worthless before God, we will be like that. We cannot be what we do not think we are. It is important to view ourselves as valued children of the Most high God. Our Father is creator of the universe. No one is greater than Him. If we concentrate on the problems we are facing , and not on our great God, we will lose it. God is greater than everything on earth. There is no problem, sickness or any other obstacle that can hinder God from making you what He wants you to be.

We are not just forgiven sinners, but we are saints. We were sinners before we repented, but after having accepted Lord Jesus Christ as our Personal Lord and Saviour, we are new creations. **2 Corinthians 5:17** "Therefore if anyone is in Christ, he is a new creation, the old has gone, the new has come." In Christ we are the children of God. We are washed by the blood of Jesus Christ.

In Christ we are under the new law of grace, the law of love. If we can take or adopt the love that our Lord has for us, then we will understand who we are in Him. We must not let the enemy whisper in our ears and deceiving us who we are in Christ. The Bible says the devil is roaring like a lion trying to get whom he can devour.

1 Peter 5:8 "Be self-controlled and alert. Your enemy the devil prowls around like a roaring lion looking for someone to devour. Resist him, stand firm in the faith, because you know that your brothers throughout the world are undergoing the same kind of sufferings." The enemy is not relaxing; he is looking for who he can get. His strategy will always be to deceive Christians.

God has given us the authority over all powers of the enemy. **Luke 10:18** "He replied, 'I saw Satan fall like lighting from heaven. I have given you the authority to trample the snakes and scorpions and to overcome all the power of the enemy; nothing will harm you.'" As long as we do not acknowledge the authority we are given, the enemy will always trouble us. The enemy does not give up, as the Bible said in **1 Peter 5:8** that he prowls like a roaring lion.

We must have faith in the authority we are given. Sometimes we are unable to face even simple problems, because of lack of faith. The spirit of fear dominates the spirit of faith we have.

Let us pray: Father in the Name of our Lord and Saviour, Jesus Christ, forgive me for not listening when you talk to me. In your Word You said, "When we come to you we are new creations, the old things are gone." As I came to you and repented I am now new before your eyes. Help me dear Lord, not to allow spirit of bondage to torment me. Help me to use the authority You have given me to command all evil spirits to leave me and my family right now in Jesus' Name – Amen.

CHAPTER SIX

STRONGHOLDS

Strongholds are high levels of demonic influence in any area(s) of the spiritual faculties of an individual. Our spiritual faculties consist of our minds, our emotions, and our will power. Spiritual strongholds are strongly established in sinful ways, false beliefs, and behaviours that have gained a strong influence over a person to the extent that each stronghold "sets itself up against the knowledge of God" (Eric Gondwe).

In areas where the strongholds are established, an individual is either unable to consistently follow God's Word or is unable to accept it, because these spiritual strongholds have an excessive influence on him.

2 Corinthians 10:3- 6 is the chapter that addresses the issue of strongholds. "For though we live in the world, we do not wage war as the world does. The weapons we fight with are not the weapons of the world. On the contrary, they have divine power to demolish **strongholds**. We demolish arguments and every pretension that sets itself up against the knowledge of God, and we take captive every thought to make it obedient to Christ. And we will be ready to punish every act of disobedience, once your obedience is complete."

Strongholds are divinely demolishable through our indirect weapons of spiritual warfare and deliverance. They are not demolished by directly confronting certain assumed spirits in geographical territories familiar spirits, generation spirits, Jezebel spirits, spirits of division, spirits of unforgiveness, spirits of addiction, etc.

Verse (5): "We demolish arguments and every pretension that sets itself up against the knowledge of God, and we take captive every thought to make it obedient to Christ. And we will be ready to punish every act of disobedience, once your obedience is complete."

For our obedience to be complete, we must always be in prayer. Prayer is the only weapon that can help our obedience to be complete. God needs our obedience so that we can fellowship with him. Obedience is better than sacrifice. King Saul was rejected by God because of lack of obedience. First he was anointed king of Israel and was instructed by God to completely destroy the Amalechites who were wicked in the eyes of the Lord. He did not obey the Lord, because he brought back king Agog. This was not what God had told him to do. He was supposed to destroy everything.

He made sacrifices from the sheep taken from the Amalechites. **1 Samuel 15:22** "But Samuel replied: 'Does the

Lord delight in burnt offerings and sacrifices as much as in obeying the voice of the Lord? To obey is better than sacrifice..." The Lord wants our obedience, and with our complete obedience we can punish every act of disobedience.

Known and unknown strongholds

The most spiritual strongholds to unbelievers are centred in removing the veil that covers the salvation of gospel. This veil is removed by God by the power of the Holy Spirit. God uses Christians to minister gospel to them and the Holy Spirit does the work.

The veils on the lives of Christians are the strongholds that hinder Christians from living true Christian lives. These strongholds are sins which are known and ignorance which is unknown and hidden.

Christians commit sins that they know are forbidden and not acceptable. They proceed to commit them again and again, and this shows that they have strongholds that need to be addressed.

Strongholds of ignorance make Christians resist the gospel. Christians of today do not know how to differentiate from ministers who deceive them and ministers who preach true gospel. This is ignorance.

To deal strongholds we must ask God to search our hearts, **Psalm 139: 23-24** "Search me O God, and know my heart; test me and know my anxious thoughts. See if there is any offensive way in me, and lead me in the way everlasting."

Christians must not forget that they have been equipped to overcome Satan's power. We are given authority to use the name of Jesus to expel the forces of evil.

How to break Strongholds and keep them broken: (Dale A. Robbins)

Authority: Every believer has the right to use the name of Jesus Christ to bind and use the authority we got from Jesus over Satan's activities. **Mark 3:27;** "No one can enter man's house and plunder his goods, unless he first binds the strong man, and then he will plunder the house."

Intercession: Come together with other believers to pray and intercede against strongholds until you get results.

Displacement: Establish the presence of God. Where Satan has been commanded to leave, fill the gap with God's presence. The devil cannot be in the presence of God. Satan does not want to hang around where people are lifting up Jesus in worship, in singing and prayer. Presence of the Lord displaces the Devil.

Resistance: We must submit ourselves and draw close to God. The Devil runs from submitted, yielded Christians James 4:7 "Therefore submit to God. Resist the devil and he will flee from you."

Occupation: Give no place or vacancy to the Devil. With the Devil departed, fill the void with God. Provide no pocket of rebellion, corruption or immorality in which Satan can find refuge to rebuild his influence or strength. **Ephesians 4:27** "Give no place to the Devil."

Fortification: Clothe yourself with God's armour. "Put on the whole armour of God, that you may be able to stand against the wiles of the devil" (**Ephesians 6:11**).

Let us pray: Lord You are the only Omnipotent God, Omnipowerful God and the almighty one. Whatever comes up in the name of stronghold is not powerful as you are. I thank you for the weapons you have given me to fight any stronghold that can come in my way. In the powerful Name of our Lord and Saviour Jesus Christ, I ask you to increase my faith to see where strongholds and weak spots are. Your say let the weak say I am strong and let the sick say I am healed. "For when I am weak, then I am strong" (2 Corinthians 12:10). I asking all these in Jesus' name – Amen.

CHAPTER SEVEN

SOUL TIES

A Soul tie is formed when you are extremely close to someone or something, i.e. best friends, or your car that you must wash every week. It is like a bridge between a person and another person, or animal of object. It is more between person and person. Anything that can cause you to think that you cannot live without it. A soul tie is also formed with every person you have had sex with. Soul ties can be formed Godly and ungodly with our family, friends, pastors, other Christians, churches, movie stars, and rock stars and other thing or somebody of more influence on our lives.

King David and Jonathan, son of Saul had a friendly soul tie. "When David had finished speaking to Saul, the soul of Jonathan was knit with the soul of David, and Jonathan loved him as his own life" (**1 Samuel 18:1**). When we choose friends, we must be careful because we may have a soul tie with someone who is not regenerated, who does not love the Lord and who does not love his neighbours just as he loves himself.

David and Jonathan formed a covenant because they loved each other so deeply. Their bond was so strong that only death could part them. **1 Samuel 18:3-4** "And Jonathan made a covenant with David because he loved him as himself. Jonathan took off the robe he was wearing and gave it to David, along with his tunic, and even his sword, his bow and his belt."

Jonathan loved David in such a way that he even told him the intentions of his father Saul. Saul became jealous of David, and he intended to kill him. **1 Samuel 18:28** "When Saul realized that the Lord was with David and his daughter Michal loved David, Saul became still more afraid of him, and he remained his enemy the rest of his days." **Chapter 19 verse 1** "Saul told his son Jonathan and all the intentions to kill David. But Jonathan was very fond of David and warned him."

In the Old Testament, people had soul tie with God. This is the soul tie we must have with our God. **Deuteronomy 10:20** "Fear the Lord your God and serve Him. Hold fast to Him and take your oaths in His name." We are to hold on our Lord on daily basis. We must commit ourselves to Him and serve Him. It is good to have soul ties with our Lord, our Heavenly Father rather than to have soul ties with the Devil. Having soul ties with God will deliver us from evil because Satan cannot stay where the Holy Spirit is.

Soul ties can be made with Christians. "For He makes the whole body fit together perfectly. As each part does its own special work, it helps the other parts grow, so that the whole body is healthy and growing and full of love." This is where the church, in all its various parts, is knitted together" **(Ephesians 4:16)**. In Colossians it reads "My purpose is that they may be encouraged in heart and united in love, so that they may have the full riches of complete understanding, in order that they may know the mystery of God, namely, Christ in whom are hidden all the treasures of wisdom and knowledge" (**Colossians 2:2**).

Godly Christian soul tie is part of God's plan, so that we can love each other and help one another. **Galatians 6:2** "Share each other's burdens, and in this way obey the law of Christ." The law of the Lord is to love our Lord with all our heart, our soul and our strength. And again we must love our neighbours as we love ourselves. **Romans 13:10** "Love does no wrong to others, so love fulfils the requirements of God's law." If our soul is tied to other Christians we would not owe them anything except love. **Romans 13:8-9** "Owe nothing to anyone—except for your obligation to love one another. If you love your neighbour, you will fulfil the requirements of God's law. For the commandments say, "You must not commit adultery. You must not murder. You must not steal. You must not covet." These—and other such commandments—are summed up in this one commandment: "Love your neighbour as yourself."

Soul tie with pastors or leaders: "So all the men of Israel withdrew from David and followed Sheba son of Bichri: but the men of Judah stayed faithfully with their king from the Jordan to Jerusalem" (**2 Samuel 20:2**).Faithful members who have a soul tie with their pastor will always be with their pastors. We are to respect anointed men of God. Pastors as shepherds must have the heart for their sheep.

Husbands and wives have a great soul tie that was tied by God Himself in the beginning. "Therefore a man shall leave his father and his mother and shall become united and cleave to his wife and they shall become one flesh" (**Genesis 2:24**). If people become one flesh, it means whatever they do is regarded as one. In case of husbands and wives, when one feels sad about something or when one is not happy, the other one is affected. They share everything, even the emotions.

This type of a soul tie is the one that make couples share everything. When one is sick, the soul of the other one also becomes affected. This reminds me of my case. My husband got sick in 2009. He was in terrible pain of appendix which was ruptured with abscess inside. The doctor who referred him to hospital did not tell him that he had only a 35% chance of living. Before he could be admitted in hospital he was unable to walk or sit down or stand up. A wheelchair was ordered to the suite where he was but unfortunately, the wheelchair could not help. We had to walk from the doctor's suite to the reception where he was supposed to be admitted.

He could not walk but he tried in those terrible pains holding on my shoulder just to arrive there. When we arrived there, the nurses rush to help me as they thought I was the one who is sick. I told them that I am not the one who is sick but my husband. They were shocked and they asked me why I looked to so terrible as if I am the one who is sick. I said to them "soul tie." I explained to them that we are sharing one special thing. Our souls are tied.

Every time when I come to visit him, they would laugh and ask me if I still feel the pain he was feeling. Then I would say to them that 'because he is no more in those terrible pains, I am also feeling better.'

One couple requested me and my prayer partners to pray for them as they were experiencing problems. The husband was also sick with something moving in his stomach. We prayed for the couple and command the sickness to leave the husband in the name of Jesus Christ.

The following day the husband experience terrible pains on the stomach and the funny part is that the wife also experience those pains. The following day when we come to check them, the wife was complaining about the pains that tormented her husband and stated that she also experienced those pains. One of my prayer partners explained to her that their souls are tied. They share everything even the pains.

There are different soul ties we can talk about. Children and parents also have soul ties like the one of Jacob and Benjamin. **Genesis 44:20** "....we have an aged father, and there is a young son born to him in his old age. His brother is dead, and he is the only one of his mother's sons left, and his father loves him." Jacob loved Benjamin because he was born to him in his old age. Normally children of the parent who are born when they are old, they become connected to their parents in such a way that parents do not want to part with them.

In **verse 30-31** it reads "So now, if the boy is not with us when I go back to your servant my father and if my father, whose life is closely bound up with the boy's life, sees that the boy isn't there, he will die." Soul ties can make one die. Joseph's bothers, not knowing that they were talking to their brother Joseph, were afraid that if they do not come back with

Benjamin to their father, their father will die because of the soul tie of their father to Benjamin.

It takes people that have a pure and giving heart that put their love in action. We must be careful of people with whom we enter into relationships . **Proverbs 1:10** "My child, if sinners entice you, turn your back on them." **Verse 15** warns us not to walk along with them. "My child, don't go along with them! Stay far away from their paths.

Soul ties can be a tremendous blessing for fellowship and growth in the Lord, but they can also be used for the devil's advantage. Just as souls can be knit or made to cleave together in a covenant relationship, they can also be tied or knit together to form bondage and enslavement.

Sexual union was ordained by God to make married partners one flesh before God, but extramarital affairs tie one soul to other partners. This is a spiritual tie between two people. Since the sexual union of marriage ties two souls together as one, if people commit fornication or adultery with one another outside their marriage, they cleave together just as in marriage. This soul tie can be stronger than the one formed through marriage.

It is important that married couples be satisfied in their sexual life. If one is not they may strongly tempted to seek sexual fulfilment elsewhere. If we become tempted and start thinking about something we shouldn't, a picture will develop in our mind, and eventually it will manifest in our lives.

Married couples must be mutually satisfied. The satisfaction must not be one-sided. The married couples must give themselves to one another and they must live to satisfy each others' needs. Couples must not be self-centred. They must not be self-serving. They must not have their standards first. They must please each other so that they can be all-satisfied. One must give him/herself to receive. This is an exchange program.

The Bible teaches us "Do not deprive each other, except by mutual consent, and for a time so that you may devote yourselves to prayer. Then come together again, so that Satan will not tempt you because of your lack of self-control" (**1 Corinthians 7:5**).

Soul ties formed from sex outside marriage causes a person to become defiled. This bond is so strong that even after many years of being involved sexually with someone outside marriage, a person may still think of their first lover. This happens because there is still a soul tie that was not renounced.

God designed every woman in such a way that the first man who has sex with her takes a form of dominion over her. "To woman he said, I will greatly increase your pains in child bearing; with pain you will give birth to children. Your desire will be for you husband, and he will rule over you." (**Genesis 3:16).**

Women do not understand why they tolerate the abuse of any kind. This is because of the soul ties. The dominion a soul tie gives a man over his lover is often so binding that he can insult and mistreat her, but she seems helplessly enslaved to him. The women end up hating themselves, because they don't understand about soul ties.

Women must be careful. Sometimes they are unable to give themselves fully to their husbands because their spirits and emotions are being continually drawn back to their past lovers. If a woman has had sexual relations with several men, her spirit and soul seek out every one of them. Her spirit is scattered and torn apart.

A man is built so that when he has sexual intimacy with a woman, his spirit wants to protect, bless, nurture and provide for that woman. That is why some men who are divorced and who remarried because they still want to protect and provide for their ex-wives.

We must ask our Lord Jesus Christ to set us free, because now we know where the problem lies in giving each other in marriage. We know the spiritual truth. We must flee form fornication. **1 Corinthians 6:18-19** "Flee from sexual immorality. All other sins a man commits are outside his body, but he who sins sexually sins against his own body. Do you not know that your body is a temple of the Holy Spirit, who is in you, whom you have received from God? You are not on your own."

This is the spirit that the Devil uses to break the family. Married couples with the problems of sexual soul ties are having problems of sexual satisfaction and this end up in divorce. Couples break up thinking they will get satisfaction somewhere else. Until this spirit is renounced and married couples give themselves to each other, people will not live in peace.

Breaking the soul ties of those old relationships can actually save our marriage, because now we are able to freely love our spouse with all our hearts. We must tie our souls fully to Christ. We must renew and strengthen those ties by communion and walk with Holy Spirit.

Breaking soul ties

We must repent from any sins that involve that person: If you have had adultery, fornication, etc, it is important that you repent of those sins and receive God's forgiveness for it before you can go about breaking the soul tie.

Forgive the person for any wrongs done: If you have any unforgiveness in your heart against the person, you must choose to release that bitterness and forgive the person. This is the bitterness discussed in previous chapters.

Renounce any covenants made with the person: If you have made any spoken commitments, vows or even simply saying, "I will love you forever", is has ample power in the spiritual realm to bind the soul to that person. The tongue is quite capable of binding the soul and can be a great means to create soul ties. **Proverbs 6:2** "If you have been trapped by what you said, ensnared by the word of your mouth, then do this my son, to free yourself.....go and humble yourself."

Get rid of any gifts exchanged: Gifts also symbolize a relationship and can hold a soul tie in place. If person has a ring, personal gifts, cards, jewellery, and other relationship gifts' from a previous relationship, then it is time to get rid of them. Holding onto such gifts symbolizes that the relationship is still in good standing and can actually hold the soul tie in place even after it has been renounced.

Renounce and break the soul tie in Jesus' Name: Verbally renouncing something carries a lot of weight in the Spiritual realm. Just as vows can bind the soul, renouncing can release the soul from bonds. Jesus said that whatsoever you shall loose will be loosed in heaven (heavenly realm, or spiritual realm).

We must ask the Lord in prayer to show us if we have bad soul ties that need to be severed. If the Lord brings people to mind or we think there are possibilities of soul ties, we must proceed to pray to cut the soul ties.

Good soul ties will bear good fruits; examples being love, blessings, fidelity, loyalty, honour, righteousness, etc. Bad soul ties will bear bad fruits for example, hatred, resentment, curses   manipulation, anger, strife, jealousy, control, bitterness, etc. The overall effect of bad soul ties will be hold us back from enjoying our relationship with God and to keep us in bondage to whatever we struggle with.

We thank our Lord for being so wonderful to teach us about all these things. Lord we adore you and we love the Holy Spirit. We adore you, Jesus< we adore you. Thank you for being so awesome and we believe as we are now going to renounce and cut the soul ties, you are going to lead and help us in Jesus' Name.

Let us pray: Dear Heavenly Father, I thank you for saving me from destruction. I praise you for sending your only Son Jesus Christ to die for my sins. Please Lord; forgive me for my sins against you. Specifically, I confess that I_____ (details of the sin & names of people your soul is tied to). I repent of that sin and renounce it now in the Name of Jesus Christ. Lord, please purify my heart from this sin, the memory of it and any associated fantasy I have entertained in my mind regarding it. In the name of our wonderful Lord Jesus Christ and by the power of his blood shed on the cross, I cut myself free from any soul ties that may have been established with_____(Names of specific objects). I commit him/ her to the care of Jesus Christ for him to do with as he wills. Satan, I rebuke you in all your works and way in Jesus' Name. I rebuke any evil Spirits that have a foothold in me. In the Name of Jesus Christ, I command you evil spirits to leave me and go directly to bottomless pit. Father, please heal my soul of any wounds resulting from these soul ties.

Please Lord reintegrates any part of me that may have been detained through this or these souls ties and restore me to wholeness. I also ask that you will reintegrate any part of the person(s) I sinned with that has been detained in me, and restore them to wholeness.

Thank you, Lord for your healing power and your perfect love for me. May I glorify you with my life from this point forward. Lord please; help me to do everything according to your will. Help me my Lord to be a good vessel that can be used by you in every manner. Help me Lord to glorify you with my tongue, my hands, my body, and in everything I do in Jesus' Name. I surrender myself to you My Lord. I surrender my blessings to you and help me to serve you in every day of my life in Jesus' Name. Amen.

Sometimes, if we feel uncomfortable cutting these soul ties for ourselves, we can ask God to cut them for us.

Let us pray this prayer: Dear Heavenly Father, I thank you for saving me from destruction. I praise you for sending your only Son Jesus Christ to die for my sins. Please Lord, forgive me for my sins against you. Specifically, I confess that I am still soul tied to _____ (details of the sin & names of people your soul is tied to). I repent of that sin and renounce it now in the Name of Jesus Christ. Please forgive me and cleanse my conscience with the blood of Jesus Christ. Lord, please cut the unhealthy soul ties between me and_____ (list the names). Please restore me to *wholeness in spirit, soul and body and reintegrate any part of me that was involved with those soul ties. I also ask for the salvation and restoration of those people that I was involved with. I commit him/ her/ them to your care. I rebuke any evil spirits that may have gained a foothold in me from that sin. I command you to leave me now in Jesus name.*

Thank you, Lord, for setting me free to live as the new person in Christ you made me to be. Thank you, Lord for your healing power and your perfect love for me. May I glorify you with my life from this point forward. Lord please; help me to do everything according to your will. Help me my Lord to be a good vessel that can be used by you in every manner. Help me Lord to glorify you with my tongue, my hands, and my body and in everything I do in Jesus' Name. I surrender myself to you My Lord. I surrender my blessings to you and help me to serve you in every day of my life in Jesus' Name. I praise you now and forever in Jesus Name, Amen.

CHAPTER EIGHT

DEVIL'S LEGAL RIGHTS/ THE PRIDE OF THE DEVIL

These are the rights that the Devil holds on Christians when he wants to torment them. He is proud of these and called them his rights. In most instances, Christians live their lives holding back some of their **sins** not confessed. This is what the Devil holds onto to claim that he still has rights on the child of God.

In this manner, our Lord is unable to help us because of the rights of the Devil or the rights the Devil is claiming in us. Some of the sins we may be aware of and others we may not. When we commit these sins we are giving the Devil the legal rights to say it proudly that we are his. He says this because he knows that all sins belong to him. It is important that if we are aware of those sins, we confess them and repent.

The hands of our Lord are open at all times waiting for us, His children, to turn to him and to shun the evil. We must verbally confess our sins and God will forgive us, and the Devil will flee from us.

Soul ties: These are destructive and most of them are formed during adultery or fornication. The Devil uses these ties to torment Christians, especially those who do not know how to get rid of these soul ties. These soul ties are like rope between two persons that demons can use to their advantages to cross from one person to another. The demons tormenting the person you have soul tie with can also torment you.

Demonic vows: These are the vows that were made consciously or unconsciously. They happen when people join cult coven (groups of witches). The vow is made with the devil. Christians should not make vows at all, except when the couple is getting married. If these vows are made, we need to repent and renounce those vows,

Unforgiveness: In most cases, people are not healed because of unforgiveness. People with unforgiving spirit in their hearts find it difficult to respond to medication. **Proverbs 17:22** "A cheerful heart is a good medicine but a crushed spirit dries up the bones."

Spoken self-curses: The words we say must be to bless and not to curse, and the tongue has the power of life and death. It is important to check what we say towards ourselves and our family members. For example people like to say "I wish I could die." This gives a legal right to devil, he can capitalize on it and the spirit of death may start to torment you. We must take back what we spoke against ourselves and renounce it. We must repent from speaking such words and start to speak blessing words and also bless others.

Points of weaknesses: When the person experience weakness, such as emotional shock, physical trauma, fearful experiences during childhood. If there is any bitterness involved, there must be forgiveness for the people who hurt you. Turning to God and asking for forgiveness is important.

Let us pray: Dear heavenly Father as I turn to You, I ask for forgiveness and I renounce all legal rights the devil may have on me. In the Name of Our Lord Jesus Christ I confess with my mouth that I do not belong to the devil, I belong to my Father who created heavens and earth. I thank you my Lord for being merciful to me and for making me the new creation in Jesus' Name, Amen.

CHAPTER NINE

THE LOVE OF MONEY/ THE SPIRIT OF MAMMON / GREEDINESS

We must not allow finances to hinder our prayers. Finance is a problem nowadays in our society. People want money in such a way that they tend to forget that God is the giver of everything. **Psalm 24:1** "The earth is the Lord's and everything in it, the world, and all who live in it." If we consider that everything on earth is of the Lord, we will not get it hard to forgive our employers if things are not going well with our finances. If we do not forgive our employers and try to pray for another job, God will not answer our prayers for unforgiveness. We must forgive our employers, pray for them, and God will meet our needs.

It is important to let God control our finances. We must not worry about other things. **Matthew 6:31-33** "Therefore take no thought, saying, what shall we eat? or, what shall we drink? or wherewithal shall we be clothed? (For after all these things do the Gentiles seek) for your heavenly Father knoweth that ye shall have need of all these things. But seek ye first the Kingdom of God, and his righteousness; and all these things shall be added unto you."

It is important to follow the law of the Lord that will make us free from the spirit of the love of money. **1Timothy 6:10-11** "For the love of money is a root all evil: which while some coveted after, they have erred from the faith and pierced themselves through with many sorrows."

Ecclesiastes 5:10 "Whoever loves money never has money enough; whoever loves wealth is never satisfied with his income." Jesus Christ alone is enough for us. He replaces everything. He said he is the bread of life.

Matthew 6:24 "No one can serve two masters. Either he will hate the one and love the other, or he will be devoted to the one and despise the other. You cannot serve both God and money." Money can make people turn from God. People think that money is the solution of every problem. They forget that even if you have a lot of money, you cannot buy joy and happiness, or we can say money cannot buy the fruit of the spirit.

So Jesus was saying the same thing, a person cannot love God and love riches. This does not mean you have to be poor to love God, but it means that God has to be first in your life, and the money has to be a tool to be used to bring glory to God and then to be used to provide the necessities of life. A person must keep the priorities right, God first, even with riches God receives the first portion in tithes (Anthony Bertrand).

The Bible teaches us that the love of money is the sign of the last days. **2 Timothy 3:1-5** "But mark this: There will be terrible times in the last days. People will be lovers of themselves [pride], lover of money, boastful, proud, abusive, disobedient to their parents, ungrateful, unholy, without love, unforgiving, slanderous without self-control, brutal, not lovers of God, treacherous, rash, conceited, lovers of pleasure rather than lovers of God, having a form of godliness but denying its power. Having nothing to do with them."

The love of money is another weapon that the devil uses to get at Christians. The enemy deceives them by telling them that if they do not have money they are nothing. The enemy tells them that they will not be the same as other people. The enemy keeps on reminding them that because they say they are the children of God, they must possess expensive things and live luxuriously. The problem is that the enemy will never tell them that the love of money is the beginning of all evil things. The enemy will never tell them that to worship money and material things is evil and not acceptable before God.

Money can be used for great good. It is powerful and as such it must be used wisely. Loving money itself is stupid. Money is a means to an end. It is the temporary representation of value, waiting to be released to cause action and exchange of goods. The more money you have, the more good you can do and the more evil you can do. The choice is yours. Be wise, work hard, provide lots of value to your fellow humans, reap the rewards (including money) and then use that money for every good thing you can for yourself, your family and others. (Brad Homer: HomerWork LLc)

We allow ourselves to be in the position where we blame God for not blessing us and we must not hold unforgiveness. God loves us and promises to bless us according to his riches. This was addressed under the heading of anger. People are angry because they are not blessed and they cannot forgive.

It is the love of money that causes all the problems of evil. It is because of the love of money that people rob, cheat, do whatever it takes to get the promotion at work, such as lie about co-workers, take credit for the work they did not perform. What about dealing drugs and crooked law enforcement officials? The list goes on, such as pornography, prostitution, the manipulation of financial books by corporate managers. The worst and most damaging to the cause of Christ are the pastors and evangelists that abuse their position for gain. They will not preach the truth about sin, the blood of Jesus which washes away all sin, because they might lose membership and money. These activities represent a small sample of what people will do for money (Anthony Bertrand)

We must not forget the commandment of God that says we must not worship any other god. Let money not take our focus from God. We must allow God to take our focus from money. Let us try to focus on the one who is everything we need. Even if we do need money, God is enough for us to get money.

Let us pray: Dear heavenly Father, please remove our focus on the world things. We know that we do not belong to this world, and we must not let world things control us. We know that with You we have everything we need. Help us, Lord, to accept the entire situation as it comes. Help us to be thankful daily, as your Word in Hebrews says "Therefore, since we are receiving a kingdom that cannot be shaken, let us be thankful, and so worship God acceptably with reverence and awe, for our God is a consuming fire" **(Hebrews 12:28).** *Lord; help us to pray at all times without ceasing . Thank you for supplying all our needs according to your riches in glory. Please give us our daily bread in Jesus name, Amen.*

CHAPTER TEN

PRAISE, WORSHIP AND PRAYER

These are the powerful tools of the Christians. Every Christians must know and be familiar with how to praise, worship and pray.

Praise and worship unlock the doors that are locked. **Acts 16:23** "After they [Paul and Silas] have been severely flogged, they were thrown into prison, and the jailer was commanded to guard them carefully. Upon receiving such orders, he put them in the inner cell, and fastened their feet in the stocks." This verse gives us a picture of bondage and stronghold. The jailer locked the doors after fastening them. When the devil puts you in bondage he also locks you in a cage where you will feel that you are alone. The devil makes us feel that no one can hear us when we talk or cry. The jailer thought he had locked them in the inner cell where nobody will hear or see them. Our Lord is an omnipresent God. He is always present in our situations.

"About midnight Paul and Silas were praying and singing hymns to God, and other prisoners were listening to them." They were singing to God. It means they were singing to the relevant person and at the same time other prisoners were listening. If praise and worship make our God act, it means praise and worship can make other people act, too. If their singing was not doing something in the lives of other prisoners, they were not going to listen. Singing to God can loosen you and other people from bondage.

"Suddenly there was such a violent earthquake that the foundations of the prison were shaken." Prisons are built on strong foundations so that no one can escape when put in jail. Praise and worship are so powerful that it can shake even such strong foundations. However strong the stronghold or bondage of the devil may be, it cannot stop the power of praise, worship, and prayer.

"At once all the prison doors flew open and everybody's chains came loose." Praise, worship and prayer do not work for only the person who is praying, but they work for others. If we praise and worship while others are in bondage and sickness, their chains become loose and others get healed.

"The jailer woke up and when he saw the prison doors open, he drew his sword and was about to kill himself because he thought the prisoners had escaped." When the devil realizes that people are loosened, he intimidates people. After the devil realized that Paul, Silas and other prisoners are free, he threatened the jailer and the jailer tried to take his life.

"But Paul shouted, 'Do not harm yourself. We are all here'! The jailer called for lights, rushed in and fell trembling before Paul and Silas. After the powerful praises and worships, the devil will fall before you. When we worship in truth and spirit, the devil trembles.

He then brought them out and asked, 'Sirs, what must I do to be saved?' They replied "believe in the Lord Jesus and you will be saved – you and your household." Praise and worship lead people to salvation.

In conclusion, we must understand that our trials and tribulations can lead others to salvation. Fighting the tools of the devil with the right tools of our Lord also lead to salvation of other people.

Paul and Silas were severely beaten; their feet strongly fastened and locked in the most inner cell but because of praise and worship, people were free and saved. We must fight the devil with the right weapons and we will win this battle.

Let us pray: Dear heavenly Father, I praise You. I worship You. I thank you for giving me the opportunity of reading this book so that I understand the tools of the devil. Thank you for teaching me to fight with the right weapons. Thank you for your Son who died for us, so that we can we saved. Thank you for raising Him up from the dead so that we can have everlasting life. Thank you Jesus for giving me the authority to trample on snakes and scorpions and to overcome all the power of the enemy. Thank you Lord that nothing will harm me in the name of our Lord Jesus Christ.

"I will exalt You, my God the King, I will praise your name for ever and ever. Every day I will praise You and extol your name for ever and ever. Let every creature praise His holy name forever and ever" **(Psalm 145:1-2, 21)**. *In Jesus' name I have prayed – Amen.*

LIST OF REFERENCES

Genesis 1:1, 2:24, 3:16, 4:4-8, 14:19-22, 37:18, 39:16, 44:4-5

Exodus20:12

Deuteronomy 10:20

Joshua 1:5, 8

2 Kings 19:35

1 Samuel 15:22, 18:1,3-4, 18:28, 26:23

2 Samuel 14:20, 20:2

Job 41:34

Psalm 10:4, 24:1, 51:3-4, 66:18, 103:12, 139:23-24, 145:1-2, 21

Proverbs 1:10, 6:2;16;18, 10:12, 11:2, 12:9, 12:15, 13:10, 15:18, 15:1, 16:18, 17:22, 19:20, 22:24, 29:1

Ecclesiastes 5:10

Isaiah 1:18, 2:1-4, 14:12-15, 41:9-10

Jeremiah 29:11

Daniel 5:21

Ezekiel 28:14, 28:17, 38:26

Matthew 5:44-48, 6:12, 6:14;15, 6:24, 6:31-33, 7:21-23, 11:28-29, 18:21-22,

Matthew 18:23-35, 27:27-44

Mark 3:27, 11:25

Luke 10:18, 15:11-31, 15:20, 17:6, 22:63-65, 23:33-34

John 12:31

John 14:24, 15:12, 16:22

Acts 1:9-11, 16:23

Romans 8:1, 8:28, 13:5, 13:8-9, 13:10

1 Corinthians 6:18-19, 7:5, 10:3-6, 13:7

2 Corinthians 2:10-11, 5:17, 10:3-6, 10:12, 12:9

Galatians 6:2,3-4

Ephesians 4:16, 4:26-27, 4:31, 6:10-18, 6:11, 12

Ephesians 12:15, 4:32, 4:31-32, 6:10-18

Philippians 2:9

Colossians 2:2

1 Thessalonians 5:18

1 Timothy 6:10-11

2 Timothy 1:7, 3:1-5

Hebrews 2:7, 12:15, 12:22, 12:28, 13:17

James 1:5, 1:9, 1:20-21, 4:6, 4:7

1 Peter 5:6, 5:8

1 John 1:9

Revelation 22:1

Alfred Ells: Counselor's corner, Volume II Issue II

Answers.com

Anthony Bertrand

Betty Miller: Exposing Satan's Devices

Brad Homer: HomerWork LLc)

Dale A. Robbins

Eric Gondwe

Joyce Mayer: 2007 (The power of simple prayer)

www.hissheep.org

Wiki.answers.com

www.charminghealth.com

www.ingramcontent.com/pod-product-compliance
Lightning Source LLC
Chambersburg PA
CBHW070519030426
42337CB00016B/2016